Understanding Science

SPECIAL NEEDS SUPPORT MATERIAL
FOR BOOK 1

Carolanne Davies
Science teacher, Bryngwyn Comprehensive School, Llanelli, Dyfed

JOHN MURRAY

Acknowledgements

Thanks are due to the following who have helped in the development of this material.

Winston Thomas, BP Chemicals, Baglan Bay

The following pupils at Bryngwyn Comprehensive School: Trina, Jayne, Rachael, Maria, Beverly, Jenny, Elizabeth, Matthew, Craig, Martin, Michael and Jason

Pam Harding, Bryngwyn Comprehensive School

Kathy Thomas and Meic Rees, Felinfoel Junior School, Llanelli

Jeff Batte, Bryngwyn Comprehensive School

Dedication

To my husband Robert and my children Gemma, Marcus and Sara

BP CHEMICALS were pleased to sponsor the author during the preparation of this material as part of the BP Baglan Bay's Support to Education.

Illustrations by Sean Humphries, Ian Foulis Associates, Ainslie MacLeod and David Webb/Linden Artists

Layouts by: Mick McCarthy

The following have given permission for photographs to be reproduced:

Cover: ZEFA Picture Library; Page 20, 41, 71, 94 and 123, The Hulton-Deutsch Collection; Page 112, The Mansell Collection; Page 158, Mary Evans Picture Library.

© Carolanne Davies 1993

First published in 1993

by John Murray (Publishers) Ltd
50 Albemarle Street, London W1X 4BD

All rights reserved

Unauthorised duplication contravenes applicable laws

Typeset by Litho Link Ltd, Welshpool, Powys, Wales

Printed in Great Britain by St Edmundsbury Press Ltd, Bury St Edmunds

A CIP catalogue record for this book is available from the British Library

ISBN 0-7195-5223-0

Guide to teachers

The National Curriculum requires pupils of all abilities to have the opportunity to study the material in the Science curriculum. Many pupils, however, find the science vocabulary difficult to read and understand. This book aims to familiarise Year 7 pupils with the new words, and help them understand their meaning. Weaker pupils can then work confidently through the mainstream book alongside pupils who have a better English language background.

Tasks from the activity sheets are written in a clear structured format, with less difficult and more difficult concepts mixed together so that pupils are motivated to attempt the harder material. Concentration and stamina are built up, giving pupils a feeling of achievement. Pupils' confidence improves as their scientific knowledge and understanding increases.

The workbook format

1. **Vocabulary list, word search, fill in the blanks, jumbled up words**
   These enable pupils to read the words, write them down and recognise the words out of context. They may cover the vocabulary from one topic or a series of topics in Understanding Science Book 1. The relevant pages in the main text are noted at the top of the page.

2. **Word puddles**
   These are a random list of relevant words needed by pupils to answer specific questions. This reduces the frustration felt by pupils since they have the key words to help them express themselves on paper.

   In some cases the word puddles have been left blank, as you may feel that including the words makes the activity too easy for your pupils.

3. **Reporting experimental work**
   Word puddles with diagrams and key words help pupils express their observations from their experiments. This is important practice for Sc1.

4. **Questions**
   Questions are asked in various formats, so helping the pupils to apply their newly found knowledge.

5. **Illustrations**
   Illustrations are included in the activity sheets so that pupils can label them or colour them as they are found in the Understanding Science book. This encourages them to look at the illustrations more carefully.

6. **Crosswords and 'clozed' procedures**
   These provide fun and applications of the vocabulary.

First experiments

experiment	lumpy	colour change
mixing	colour	chemical
clear	pour	chemicals
fizzy	shake	test tube
cloudy		

Complete the word search using the words above.

e	x	p	e	r	i	m	e	n	t	a	h	m
a	b	c	y	z	z	i	f	a	e	c	a	i
c	o	l	o	u	r	b	c	d	s	h	p	x
c	h	e	m	i	c	a	l	s	t	e	p	i
n	o	t	h	i	n	g	e	f	t	m	e	n
m	r	c	l	o	u	d	y	g	u	i	n	g
c	z	p	o	u	r	h	i	j	b	c	e	s
l	u	m	p	y	k	l	c	l	e	a	r	t
s	h	a	k	e	m	n	o	p	q	l	r	u
c	o	l	o	u	r	c	h	a	n	g	e	v

UNDERSTANDING SCIENCE BOOK 1 PAGES 12-15

The following words have been put back to front. Write them the correct way.

tnemirepxe	
ebut tset	
gnixim	
lacimehc	
ypmul	
yduolc	
yzzif	
ruoloc	
ekahs	
ruop	

From the words above fill in the blanks.

l u _ _ _

f i _ _ _

c l _ _ d _

m _ x _ _ _

e x _ _ _ _ m _ n t

US 1 Support Material

UNDERSTANDING SCIENCE BOOK 1 PAGE 12

Look at the test tubes below. Which word best describes the chemicals in each of the tubes?

cloudy   fizzy   clear

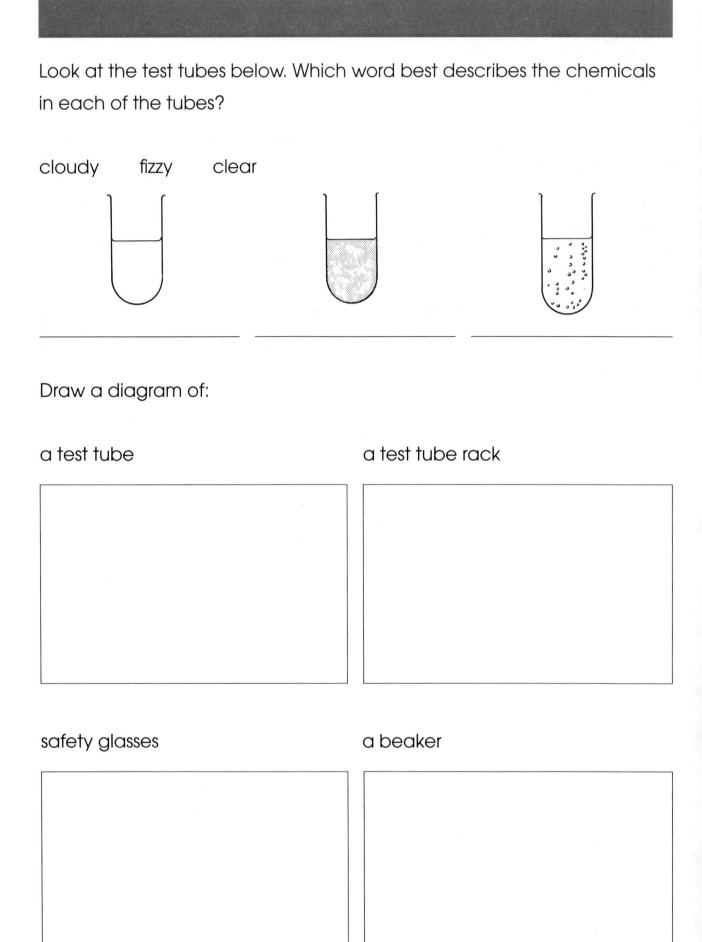

Draw a diagram of:

a test tube

a test tube rack

safety glasses

a beaker

UNDERSTANDING SCIENCE BOOK 1 PAGE 14

Reporting on an experiment

Write this in your own handwriting below.

Diagram

Method

I mixed clear sodium carbonate with blue copper sulphate.

Results

A cloudy blue mixture was seen.

Diagram

Method

Results

US 1 Support Material

UNDERSTANDING SCIENCE BOOK 1 PAGE 14

Write the results of these experiments.

1 Water movements

1 Turn the tap on so that the water is trickling out in a thin stream.

2 Rub the plastic rod very hard with the duster.

3 Hold the rod near the running water. Do not let it touch the water.

Try rubbing the rod against your jumper.

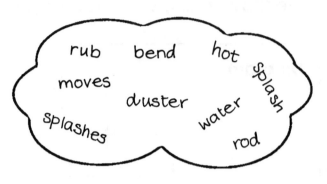

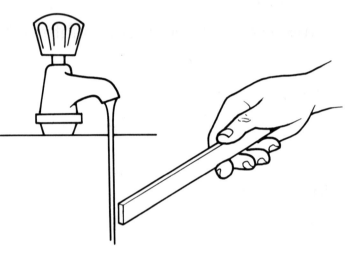

Results

_____
_____
_____

continued ➤

➤ *continued*

2 Water music

1 Half fill the beaker with water.

2 Tap the tuning fork gently on the cork mat.

3 Put the fork into the water.

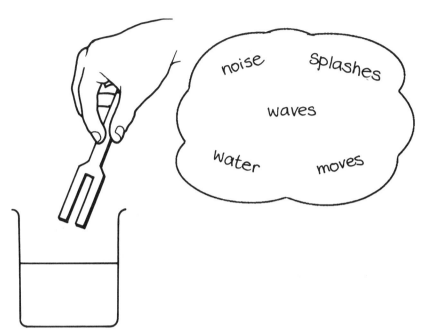

Results

_____

_____

_____

3 Vinegar drops

1 Put a piece of indicator paper on the white tile.

2 Put a drop of vinegar on the paper.

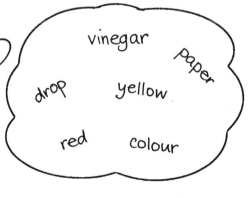

Results

_____

_____

_____

continued ➤

➤ *continued*

4 Watch the birdie

1. Hold the knitting needle between your hands as shown.

2. Rub your hands together backwards and forwards. The needle will twirl.

3. Look at the picture card while you do this.

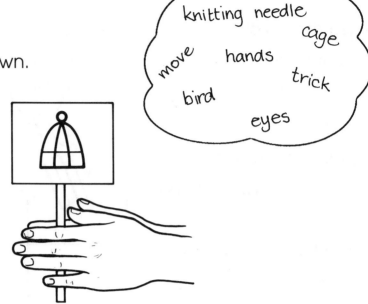

Results

_____

_____

_____

5 Fizzy veg

1. Add a little clear liquid to a test tube.

2. Put a little chopped potato into the clear liquid.

3. Clean the test tube afterwards.

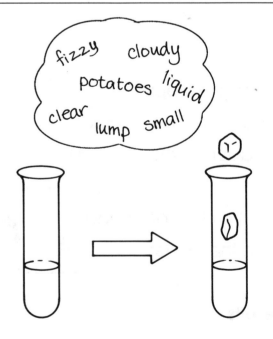

Results

_____

_____

_____

continued ➤

➤ *continued*

6 Seeing sound

1 Look at the little screen.

2 Put your mouth close to the microphone.

3 Make a loud high noise. For example, whistle.

4 Make a low noise now.

Results

_____
_____
_____

UNDERSTANDING SCIENCE BOOK 1 PAGES 16-20

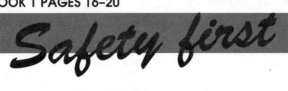

science	fire	barrel
scientist	flame	base
science room	rubber tubing	collar
safety	air hole	safety glasses

Complete the word search using the words above.

a	s	c	i	e	n	c	e	a	b	c	d	e	f
s	c	i	e	n	c	e	r	o	o	m	i	l	k
c	r	u	b	b	e	r	t	u	b	i	n	g	j
i	a	b	c	d	e	f	b	a	s	e	g	h	i
e	m	n	o	p	q	r	s	t	c	u	v	w	x
n	s	a	f	e	t	y	y	z	o	a	b	c	d
t	e	f	g	b	a	r	r	e	l	h	i	j	k
i	l	m	n	a	i	r	h	o	l	e	o	p	q
s	r	e	s	t	u	v	w	x	a	y	z	a	b
t	a	m	b	c	d	e	f	i	r	e	f	g	h
i	j	a	k	l	m	n	n	o	p	q	r	s	t
u	v	l	w	x	y	z	a	b	c	d	e	f	g
s	a	f	e	t	y	g	l	a	s	s	e	s	h

UNDERSTANDING SCIENCE BOOK 1 PAGES 16-20

The following words have been put back to front. Write them the correct way.

ytefas	
sessalg	
erif	
emalf	
ralloc	
lerrab	
esab	
regnad	
tnilps	
tsitneics	

From the words above fill in the blanks.

s _ f _ _ _

f i _ _

c o _ _ _ _

d _ _ g _ _

s _ _ _ _ _ i s t

Bunsen burner

Label the diagram below.

collar barrel base air hole rubber tubing mat

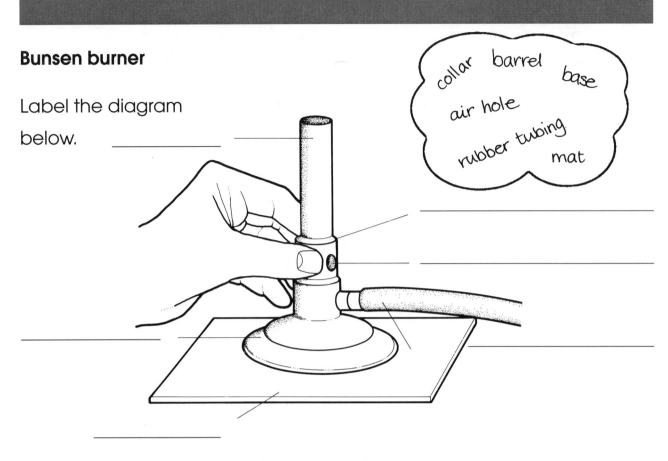

Using your yellow and blue felt pens, colour in the flame when:

air hole closed

safe flame

air hole open

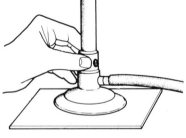

very hot flame

UNDERSTANDING SCIENCE BOOK 1 PAGE 16

Write a report of your experiment.

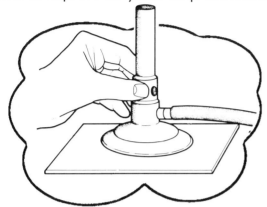 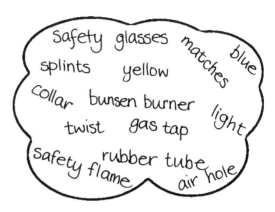

Diagram

Method

_____
_____
_____
_____

Results

When the air hole was closed we had a _____ coloured flame.

When the air hole was open we had a _____ coloured flame.

UNDERSTANDING SCIENCE BOOK 1 PAGE 17

Look at each of the pictures below and write a sentence to say what the danger is. (Colour in the pictures.)

_____   _____
_____   _____
_____   _____
_____   _____

_____   _____
_____   _____
_____   _____
_____   _____

Design a sign

flammable	foreign	definition
poisonous	shipment	personal
explosive	solve	history
chemicals	kill	file

Complete the word search using the words above.

a	f	l	a	m	m	a	b	l	e	e	a	c	s
p	o	i	s	o	n	o	u	s	o	l	v	e	c
b	r	s	h	i	p	m	e	n	t	c	a	r	e
p	e	r	s	o	n	a	l	s	a	f	e	s	a
h	i	s	t	o	r	y	f	i	l	e	n	o	b
a	g	a	b	e	x	p	l	o	s	i	v	e	e
a	n	a	b	c	h	e	l	l	o	y	o	u	f
b	k	w	h	a	t	i	s	y	o	u	r	s	e
c	i	n	a	m	e	l	t	h	a	b	c	c	e
d	l	a	c	d	e	f	i	n	i	t	i	o	n
e	l	s	l	a	c	i	m	e	h	c	a	b	c

UNDERSTANDING SCIENCE BOOK 1 PAGE 18

The following words have been put back to front. Write them the correct way.

elbammalf	
suonosiop	
evisolpxe	
slacimehc	
ngierof	
tnempihs	
evlos	
llik	
noitinifed	
lanosrep	

From the words above fill in the blanks.

f l _ _ _ _ _ l e

p o _ _ _ _ _ u s

e x _ _ _ s _ _ _

k _ _ _

s _ _ v _

Underline the correct answer.

Flammable means: it will blow up

it will catch fire easily

it will kill you if you eat it

Poisonous means: it will blow up

it will catch fire easily

it will kill you if you eat it

Explosive means: it will blow up

it will catch fire easily

it will kill you if you eat it

Draw pictures instead of words for the labels of the boxes below.

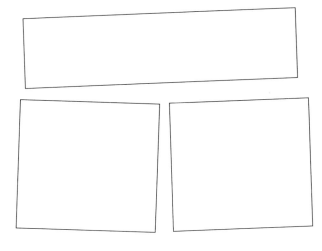

Crossword

1 Worn in the lab to stop you hurting your eyes.

2 Colour of a safe bunsen flame.

3 If you put glass into a 'paper only' bin this could happen.

4 If you were to eat in the lab this could happen.

UNDERSTANDING SCIENCE BOOK 1 PAGE 19

Talkabout

Life in 2020 AD

Write three sentences about school life in the year 2020.

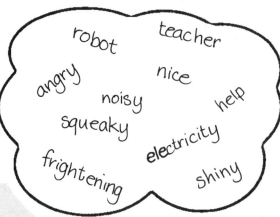

UNDERSTANDING SCIENCE BOOK 1 PAGE 20

Readabout

Alfred Nobel

Read page 20.

Name: _____
Place of birth: _____
Year of birth: _____
Three interesting facts:
_____
_____
_____

Crossword

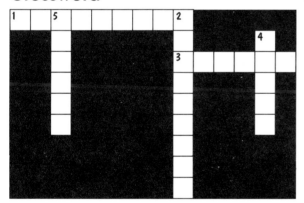

1 It will catch fire easily.
2 It will blow up.
3 It will kill you if you eat it.
4 A mechanical teacher.
5 Nobel's first name.

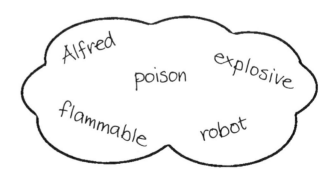

Alfred   poison   explosive   flammable   robot

Now ask to do skill sheets 1, 4, 7, 8, 10, 18.

UNDERSTANDING SCIENCE BOOK 1 PAGES 12-20

Unit 1 test

Name _____   Form _____

Read about the following experiments.

Experiment 1 Liquid A was mixed with liquid B. A white solid formed.

Experiment 2 When liquid C and liquid A were mixed nothing happened.

Experiment 3 A green solid forms when liquid D is mixed with liquid A.

1a How many liquids were there altogether? _____

b What happens when liquid A and liquid D are mixed?
_____
_____

c Which two liquids would you mix to make a white solid?
_____

d How many experiments were done altogether? _____

2 Look at the pictures below. What are the objects?

_____   _____

continued ▶

UNDERSTANDING SCIENCE BOOK 1 PAGES 12–20

➤ continued

3 Give two important safety rules.

1 _____
_____
_____

2 _____
_____

4 Label the bunsen burner.

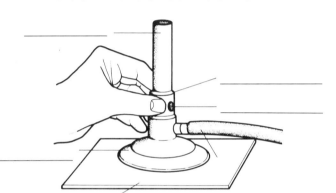

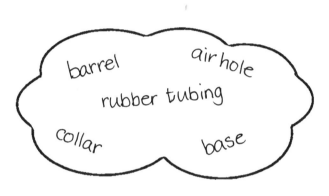

barrel   air hole
rubber tubing
collar   base

5 Put in the missing answers.

Air hole	Flame colour
open	
closed	

6 What is the name of the man in the picture?

_____
_____

Set about sets

UNDERSTANDING SCIENCE BOOK 1 PAGES 22-23

sorting	sets	shapes
objects	similar	insect
muddle	common	animal
science	exactly	birds
set	animals	pets

Complete the word search using the words above.

a	b	c	d	e	f	p	e	t	s	a	g
s	i	m	i	l	a	r	h	i	j	n	k
l	b	i	r	d	s	m	n	o	p	i	q
r	s	t	u	v	w	x	y	z	a	m	b
t	e	s	o	r	t	i	n	g	j	a	k
c	x	c	b	d	e	f	g	h	i	l	l
m	a	i	j	n	s	e	p	a	h	s	o
p	c	e	e	q	r	s	t	u	v	i	w
x	t	n	c	o	m	m	o	n	y	n	z
a	l	c	t	b	c	u	d	e	f	s	g
h	y	e	s	i	j	d	k	l	m	e	n
o	p	q	r	s	t	d	u	v	w	c	x
a	a	n	i	m	a	l	s	a	b	t	c
y	b	c	d	e	s	e	t	s	f	g	h
d	e	f	g	h	e	l	l	o	a	b	c

UNDERSTANDING SCIENCE BOOK 1 PAGES 22-23

The following words have been put back to front. Write them the correct way.

gnitros	
stcejbo	
elddum	
ecneics	
tes	
sepahs	
tcesni	
slamina	
sdrib	
step	

From the words above fill in the blanks.

s _ _

s o _ _ _ n g

m u _ _ _ _

s c _ _ _ _ _

i n _ _ _ _

UNDERSTANDING SCIENCE BOOK 1 PAGE 22

Sorting

Look at the picture of the science room on page 22.

Draw diagrams of the different objects in the science room.

| beaker | test tube | cups |

number in picture ____   number in picture ____   number in picture ____

| books | bunsen burner | tripod |

number in picture ____   number in picture ____   number in picture ____

| chemical bottle | conical flask |

number in picture ____   number in picture ____

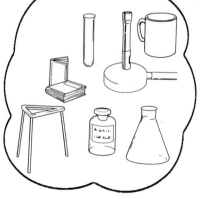

26   US 1 Support Material

Sets

Complete the sentences below using the information in the box.

> **meaning:** the same in every way.
> **meaning:** a group of things of the same kind.
> **meaning:** like something. Not exactly the same.

A set is _____

_____

Similar means _____

_____

Exactly means _____

_____

Give a name to each of the sets below.

 A set of _____

Set of birds
Set of insects
Set of animals
Set of pets

A set of _____   A set of _____   A set of _____

UNDERSTANDING SCIENCE BOOK 1 PAGES 24-27

The set of living things

born	fight	observation
breathe	run	examine
grow	toilet	conditions
move	alive	collect
eat	dead	earthworm

Complete the word search using the words above.

```
e a e c o n d i t i o n s d e f
a g x h i j k l m n o f c p q r
t s a o b s e r v a t i o n t u
v w m x o y z u a b c g l a b c
a b i c r d e n f g h h l i j k
l m n n o p q r s t t e u v w
x u e a r t h w o r m z c a b c
a b c g r o w d e f o g t h i j
k l m n o i p q d r v s t u v w
x y z a a l i v e b e c d e f g
h i j k l e m n a b r e a t h e
o r a n d t t i d n s h i j k l
```

UNDERSTANDING SCIENCE BOOK 1 PAGES 24-27

The following words have been put back to front. Write them the correct way.

nrob	
ehtaerb	
worg	
evom	
tae	
evila	
tcelloc	
noitavresbo	
daed	
enimaxe	

From the words above fill in the blanks.

a _ _ _ _

d _ _ _

o _ _ _ _ _ _ _ _ _ _

e _ _ _ _ _ _

c _ _ _ _ _ _

UNDERSTANDING SCIENCE BOOK 1 PAGE 25

> Ask for resource 2.2.

Take the pictures and make two piles.

Pile 1: living things.
Pile 2: non-living things.

List 10 of each type below.

Living	Non-living
1	
2	
3	
4	
5	
6	
7	
8	
9	
10	

UNDERSTANDING SCIENCE BOOK 1 PAGE 24-26

What living things do

Look at the cartoons on page 24.

Complete the table.

Cartoon	What all living things do
1	
2	
3	
4	
5	
6	
7	

Look at page 26.

Name the following animals.

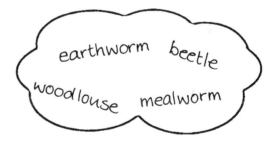

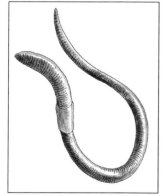 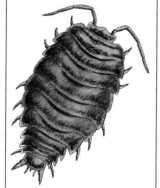  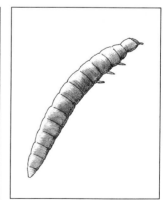

_____   _____   _____   _____

UNDERSTANDING SCIENCE BOOK 1 PAGE 27

Examining a living thing

Collect an animal.

earthworm mealworm pink
woodlouse brown black grey
mud dark brown sand
under wood soil under stones

Name of animal _____

1 How long is the animal? _____ cm

2 How wide is the animal? _____ cm

3 What is its colour? _____

4 Does it have:
   stripes
   scales
   rings?   _____

5 How many legs does it have?   _____

6 How many eyes does it have?   0   1   2   4   6

7 How many antennae are there?   0   1   2   4   6

8 How fast does it move?   fast / slow

9 Is it noisy when it moves?   yes / no

10 Where does it live?   _____

US 1 Support Material

UNDERSTANDING SCIENCE BOOK 1 PAGES 28-38

Your scientific eye

vertebrates	structure	observation
invertebrates	feeding	amphibians
observe	habitat	mammals
backbone	type	reptile
movement	animals	suckles

Complete the word search using the words above.

```
a b c d v a n i m a l s m a m m a l s
e f g h e b a c k b o n e i j k l m n
i n v e r t e b r a t e s t r u c t u
s o p q t a b c m d e f t g h i j k r
u a l m e n o p o q a b r c d b e h e
c m f o b s e r v e g h u i j a k a p
k p l m r n u p e a b c c m n c o b t
l h a b a a b c m d e f t p q k a i i
e i c d t a b c e g h i u h a b l t l
s b e f e d e f n j k l r a b o c a e
g i h i s a b c t q f e e d i n g t e
j a k l m n o p y h e l l o a e b c d
a n b c d e f g p l m n o p q r s t u
h s i j k o b s e r v a t i o n f g h
```

UNDERSTANDING SCIENCE BOOK 1 PAGES 28–38

The following words have been put back to front. Write them the correct way.

tnemevom	
tatibah	
evresbo	
gnideef	
setarbetrev	
enobkcab	
setarbetrevni	
erutcurts	
selkcus	
elitper	

From the words above fill in the blanks.

b _ _ _ b _ _ _

f. _ _ _ i n g

h _ _ _ _ a t

m o _ _ _ _ _ _

o b _ _ _ _ _

Vertebrates and invertebrates

Tick ✓ if it's true.

1 Vertebrates have a backbone. _____
2 Invertebrates have a backbone. _____
3 A fish has a backbone. _____
4 A duck has a backbone. _____
5 A worm has a backbone. _____

Look at page 29

Name five vertebrate and five invertebrate animals.

Vertebrate	Invertebrate

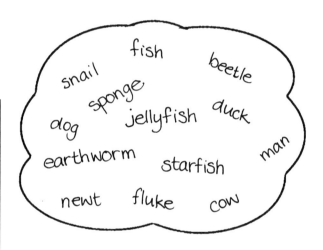

snail fish beetle
dog sponge jellyfish duck
earthworm starfish man
newt fluke cow

Why is it difficult to spot the backbones of some animals?

_____
_____
_____

scales backbone hair
covered by skin
feathers fur

UNDERSTANDING SCIENCE BOOK 1 PAGE 30

Observing an animal

Name of animal _____ size _____cm

Drawing of the animal.

Tick ✓ the correct description for the animal you are observing.

1 Movement

Speed of movement	What makes it move	Why it moves
fast _____	legs _____	to eat food _____
slow _____	fins _____	being nosey _____
still _____	tail _____	it's frightened _____
jerky _____	wings _____	going to toilet _____
smooth _____	muscles _____	being friendly _____

2 Structure

Shape		Body covering		Bits	
round	___	skin	___	mouth	___
flat	___	fur	___	ears	___
thin	___	scales	___	eyes	___
fat	___	hair	___	nose	___
square	___	sticky	___	antennae	___

3 Feeding

What it eats		How it eats	
plants	___	teeth	___
meat	___	claws	___
meat and plants	___	jaws	___

4 Habitat

Where does it live?		Conditions?	
land	___	in the dark	___
sea	___	in the light	___
river	___	in the wet	___
pond	___	in the dry	___

UNDERSTANDING SCIENCE BOOK 1 PAGE 32

Sets of vertebrates

> **Body covering:** covers the animal's body. Humans have skin, birds have feathers.

Look at the list of body coverings below.

fur   hair   feathers   scales   damp skin

What type of body covering do each of the following have?

frog _____   horse_____   crocodile _____

fish _____   bird _____   human _____

gorilla _____   chicken _____   snake _____

Eggs or live birth?

Look at the pictures here. Decide if these animals have eggs or if their babies grow inside them (live birth).

mammal

bird

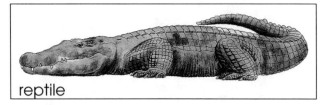
reptile

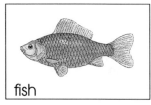
fish

frog

UNDERSTANDING SCIENCE BOOK 1 PAGE 32

Study the table below.

Groups	Name	Body covering	Warm/cold blooded	Eggs/live birth
1 mammal	horse	fur/hair	warm	live birth
2 bird	robin	feather	warm	eggs
3 fish	goldfish	scale/fins	cold	eggs
4 amphibian	frog	moist skin	cold	eggs
5 reptile	crocodile	dry scales	cold	eggs

1 Name three cold blooded groups.

   a _____

   b _____

   c _____

2 Which group has moist skin and is cold blooded? _____

3 Do fish have eggs or do their young grow inside them? _____

4 Is a bird warm or cold blooded? _____

5 What group does a horse belong to? _____

6 Give an example of an amphibian. _____

UNDERSTANDING SCIENCE BOOK 1 PAGE 35

Using keys

A key in science helps you work out, through questions and answers, what something is.

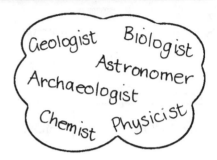

Look at page 35. Use the key to find out the name of each scientist.

_____ _____ _____

_____ _____ _____

Write three sentences about life on other planets.

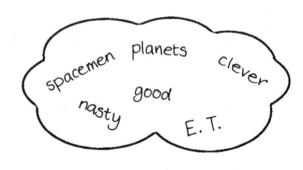

_____

_____

_____

40 US 1 Support Material

UNDERSTANDING SCIENCE BOOK 1 PAGE 38

Readabout

Charles Darwin

Read page 38.

Name: _____
Place of birth: _____
Year of birth: _____
Three interesting facts:
_____
_____
_____

Crossword

1 Has a backbone.
2 Country where Darwin was born.
3 Has feathers.
4 Warm blooded animal, live birth.
5 A scientist uses one of these to help identify unknown objects.

England   mammal   vertebrate   bird   key

Now ask to do skill sheets 12, 24, 45, 47.

US 1 Support Material

UNDERSTANDING SCIENCE BOOK 1 PAGES 22–38

Unit 2 test

Name _____ Form _____

1 Underline the odd one out in each of the lists below.

List A	List B	List C
sofa	ruler	mouse
bench	pen	house
table	crayon	louse
chair	pencil	cow

2 Look at the bottle in front of you. List three important details about the bottle.

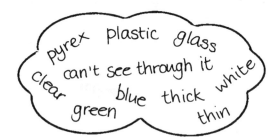

pyrex plastic glass
clear can't see through it
green blue thick white
            thin

1 _____

2 _____

3 _____

3 Name one vertebrate.

_____

4 Name one invertebrate.

_____

5 How can you tell the difference between vertebrate and invertebrate animals?

_____ _____

continued ➤

UNDERSTANDING SCIENCE BOOK 1 PAGES 22–38

➤ *continued*

6 Look at the picture below.

- **a** Are the animals in the picture all from the set of wild animals? Yes/No
- **b** Which animal in the picture above has no backbone? _____
- **c** Underline the correct answer. What is a set?

    Is it:

    things that are **exactly** the same.

    things that are **similar**?

7 Look at the set below. Name 2 animals that can be added to the set.

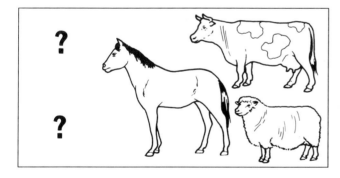

1 _____
2 _____

8 Give three ways of telling if something is alive.

1 _____
2 _____
3 _____

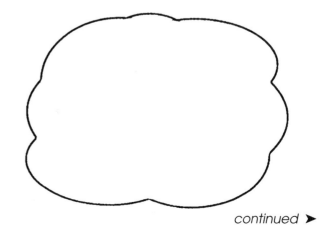

continued ➤

UNDERSTANDING SCIENCE BOOK 1 PAGES 22-38

➤ *continued*

9 Use the key to identify the animal.

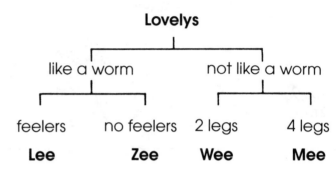

The name of the animal is _____

10 Draw a picture of Dan using the information from the key.

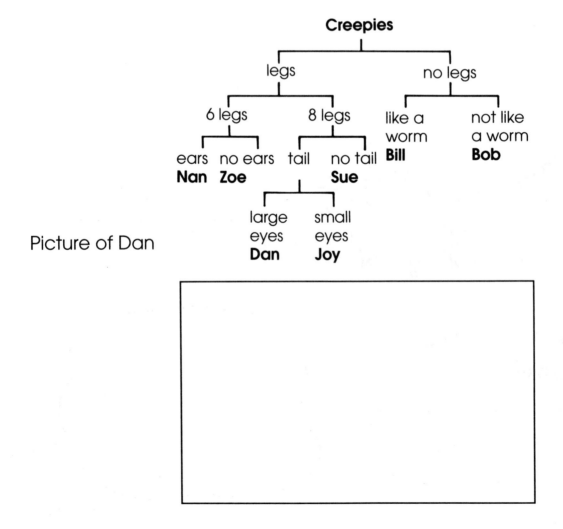

Picture of Dan

UNDERSTANDING SCIENCE BOOK 1 PAGES 40-41

Water movement

frozen	melting	gas
liquid	boiling	cycle
vapour	freezing	disappear
condensation	solid	quickly
evaporation	hot	cold

Complete the word search using the words above.

c	o	n	d	e	n	s	a	t	i	o	n
a	a	h	b	c	c	y	c	l	e	h	b
f	r	o	z	e	n	s	o	l	i	d	o
r	i	t	j	k	l	m	l	n	o	p	l
e	g	a	s	t	u	v	d	w	x	y	i
e	i	d	v	a	p	o	u	r	z	a	q
z	q	u	i	c	k	l	y	c	d	e	u
i	u	m	e	l	t	i	n	g	g	h	i
n	i	b	o	i	l	i	n	g	j	k	d
g	e	v	a	p	o	r	a	t	i	o	n
d	i	s	a	p	p	e	a	r	m	n	o

US 1 Support Material

UNDERSTANDING SCIENCE BOOK 1 PAGES 40-41

The following words have been put back to front. Write them the correct way.

nezorf	
ruopav	
gnitlem	
gniliob	
gnizeerf	
dilos	
diuqil	
sag	
elcyc	

From the words above fill in the blanks.

v _ _ o u r

b _ _ l _ _ _

f _ _ z _ _

m _ _ _ i n g

c _ c _ _

UNDERSTANDING SCIENCE BOOK 1 PAGE 41

Fill in the missing words.

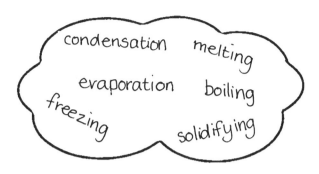

1 When a solid changes into a liquid it is called _____

2 When a liquid changes into a gas it is called _____ or _____

3 When a gas changes into a liquid it is called _____

4 When a liquid changes into a solid it is _____ or _____

Write the word that best describes what is happening to the water in each picture.

_____

_____

_____

US 1 Support Material

UNDERSTANDING SCIENCE BOOK 1 PAGE 41

Water cycle

Put the missing words into the diagram below.

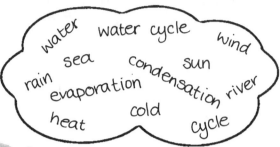

Write three sentences that explain the water cycle.

_____

_____

_____

_____

Crossword

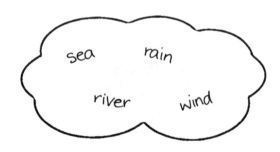

1 The sun's heat causes water to evaporate from here.

2 This blows the clouds over the mountains.

3 Water falls as this.

4 The way water travels back to the sea.

dissolving	solvent	chemical
dissolve	solution	splint
soluble	sugar	test tube
insoluble	disappear	test tube rack

Complete the word search using the words above.

i	a	s	u	g	a	e	v	l	o	s	s	i	d	d
n	s	o	l	v	e	n	t	o	n	m	l	k	i	i
s	o	l	b	c	d	e	e	f	g	h	i	j	s	s
o	l	u	a	b	c	d	s	p	l	i	n	t	a	s
l	u	t	e	f	g	h	t	i	j	k	l	m	p	o
u	b	i	v	u	t	s	t	r	q	p	o	n	p	l
b	l	o	w	x	y	s	u	g	a	r	z	a	e	v
l	e	n	b	c	d	e	b	f	g	h	i	j	a	i
e	k	l	m	n	o	p	e	q	r	s	t	u	r	n
t	e	s	t	t	u	b	e	r	a	c	k	h	a	g
c	h	e	m	i	c	a	l	a	b	c	d	e	f	g

UNDERSTANDING SCIENCE BOOK 1 PAGES 42-43

The following words have been put back to front. Write them the correct way.

evlossid	
tnevlos	
noitulos	
elbulos	
raeppasid	
ragus	
elbulosni	
lacimehc	
tnilps	
ebut tset	

From the words above fill in the blanks.

d i _ _ p p _ _ _

d i _ _ _ _ v e

s _ _ v _ _ _

s _ _ u t _ _ _

s _ _ u b _ _

Dissolving

Fill in the blanks using the words in the word puddle.

Word puddle: dissolves, soluble, solvent, disappeared

When sugar is put into a cup of tea it d _ _ _ _ l v e s.

You can taste the sugar but you cannot see it.

It seems to have d _ _ _ p p _ _ _ _ _.

Sugar is said to be s _ _ u b _ _ in the hot water.

The hot water is called the s _ _ v _ _ t.

UNDERSTANDING SCIENCE BOOK 1 PAGE 43

Testing solubility

> **soluble** — the chemical disappears in the water.
> **insoluble** — the chemical can still be seen in the water.

You will need:
- test tube rack
- four test tubes
- four corks
- beaker
- water
- wooden splint
- four watch glasses
- chemicals
- safety spectacles
- cloth

UNDERSTANDING SCIENCE BOOK 1 PAGE 43

Draw a picture of each piece of apparatus below. (The first one is done for you.)

test tube rack	test tubes
beaker with water	corked test tubes
wooden splint	watch glasses
safety spectacles	cloth

1 Put safety spectacles on.

2 Put the test tubes into the test tube rack.

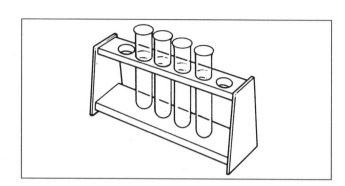

3 Take the beaker full of water and pour water into each test tube.

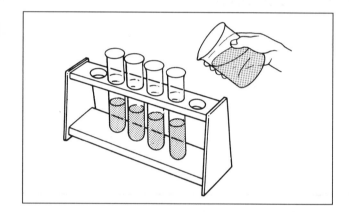

4 Take the wooden spatula and put a small amount of chemical onto it.

5 Put the chemical into the test tube.

continued ➤

➤ *continued*

6 **Place a cork on top of the test tube.**

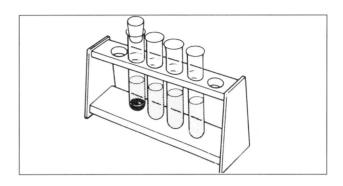

7 **Pull the test tube out of the rack and shake from side to side.**

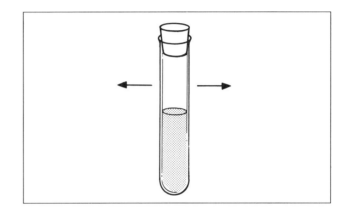

8 **Put the test tube back into the test tube rack and look to see if the chemical has disappeared.**

9 **Fill in the table below.**

Name of chemical	Chemical has disappeared	Chemical can be seen

continued ➤

UNDERSTANDING SCIENCE BOOK 1 PAGE 43

➤ *continued*

10 Try the experiment again with another chemical.

Practical marks

Safety _____

Doing the practical _____

Following instructions _____

Completing tasks _____

UNDERSTANDING SCIENCE BOOK 1 PAGES 46–47

Colourful papers

chromatography	filter paper
dyes	wick
inks	evaporating dish
mixture	beaker
colours	report

Complete the word search using the words above.

a	b	r	e	p	o	r	t	c	d	e	f	g	h	d
i	c	h	r	o	m	a	t	o	g	r	a	p	h	y
j	k	l	m	n	i	n	k	s	o	p	q	r	s	e
t	u	v	w	x	x	y	z	a	b	c	d	e	f	s
g	h	i	j	k	t	l	m	w	i	c	k	n	o	p
q	c	o	l	o	u	r	s	r	s	t	u	v	w	x
y	z	a	b	c	r	d	e	b	e	a	k	e	r	f
g	h	i	j	k	e	l	m	n	o	p	q	r	s	t
f	i	l	t	e	r	p	a	p	e	r	u	v	w	x
e	v	a	p	o	r	a	t	i	n	g	d	i	s	h
d	i	s	h	y	z	a	b	c	d	e	f	g	h	i
j	k	l	m	n	o	p	q	r	s	t	u	v	w	x

US 1 Support Material

UNDERSTANDING SCIENCE BOOK 1 PAGES 46–47

The following words have been put back to front. Write them the correct way.

yhpargotamorhc	
seyd	
rekaeb	
retlif	
gnitaropave	
sruoloc	
troper	
kciw	
erutxim	
repap	

From the words above fill in the blanks.

c h _ _ _ a _ _ _ r a _ _ _

f _ _ _ _ _ p _ _ _ _

e _ _ _ _ _ _ _ i n g

c _ _ _ _ _ _

r _ _ _ _ _

Chromatography

You will need:
- filter paper
- scissors
- beaker and water
- ink

1. Take the filter paper and put it on the bench.

2. Take some ink and put it in the middle of the filter paper.

3. Take the scissors and cut the filter paper as shown.

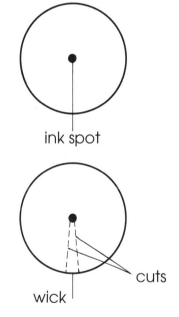

4. Bend down the cut piece of filter paper.

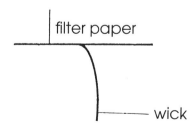

continued ➤

> *continued*

5 **Put the filter paper and wick on top of a beaker with water in it.**

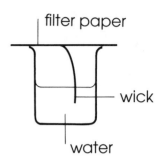

6 **Make sure the wick touches the water.**

7 **Wait.**

8 **What can you see?**
_____
_____
_____

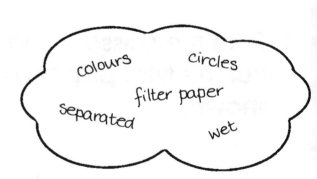

continued >

UNDERSTANDING SCIENCE BOOK 1 PAGE 46

➤ *continued*

9 Stick the filter paper on here.

Practical marks

Safety   _____

Doing the practical   _____

Following instructions   _____

Completing tasks   _____

US 1 Support Material

Write a report of your experiment.

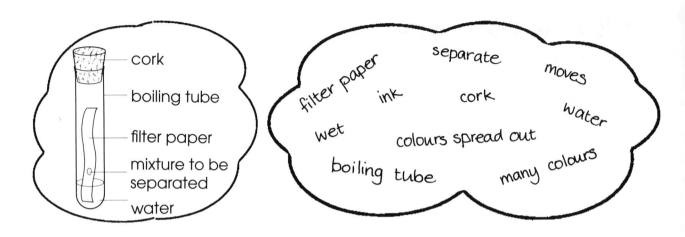

Diagram

Method

Results

UNDERSTANDING SCIENCE BOOK 1 PAGE 47

Write a report of your experiment.

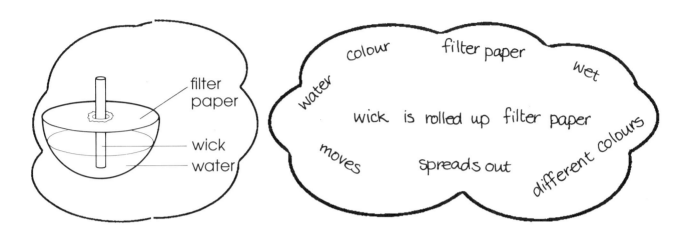

Diagram

Method

_____
_____
_____

Results

_____
_____
_____
_____

UNDERSTANDING SCIENCE BOOK 1 PAGES 48–52

Fix the mix

rock	crystals	distillation
separating	soluble	condense
mixture	evaporates	condenses
filtering	solve	insoluble
cooled	waiter	

Complete the word search using the words above.

a	b	r	o	c	k	a	c	r	y	s	t	a	l	s
s	o	l	u	b	l	e	c	d	e	f	g	h	c	o
j	i	s	e	p	a	r	a	t	i	n	g	k	o	l
e	v	a	p	o	r	a	t	e	s	l	m	n	n	v
c	q	c	o	n	d	e	n	s	e	s	o	p	d	e
o	d	i	s	t	i	l	l	a	t	i	o	n	e	y
o	r	s	t	u	r	e	t	i	a	w	v	w	n	x
l	x	m	i	x	t	u	r	e	f	g	i	k	s	z
e	v	w	y	z	a	b	c	d	e	h	j	l	e	a
d	c	o	n	d	e	n	s	e	s	n	o	p	q	b
u	i	n	s	o	l	u	b	l	e	j	k	l	m	c
s	r	d	i	s	t	i	l	l	a	t	i	o	n	d
t	f	i	l	t	e	r	i	n	g	f	g	h	i	e

UNDERSTANDING SCIENCE BOOK 1 PAGES 48-52

The following words have been put back to front. Write them the correct way.

slatsyrc	
elbulos	
delooc	
evlos	
elbulosni	
noitallitsid	
sesnednoc	
gnitarapes	
erutxim	
setaropave	

From the words above fill in the blanks.

d _ _ _ _ _ _ _ _ _ _ _

e _ _ _ _ _ _ _ _ _

s _ _ _ _ _ _ in g

m _ _ _ _ _ _

c o _ _ _ _ _ _ _

UNDERSTANDING SCIENCE BOOK 1 PAGE 48

Salt from rock

Filtering

You will need:

- filter paper
- filter funnel
- pestle/mortar
- beaker
- water
- stirrer
- test tube rack
- bunsen burner
- tripod/gauze
- evaporating dish

1 Take some filter paper. Fold the filter paper as shown.

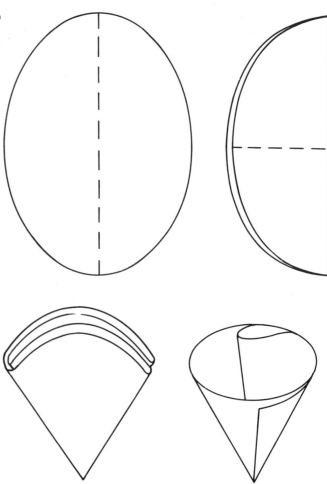

continued ➤

US 1 Support Material

➤ *continued*

2 Put the folded paper into the filter funnel.

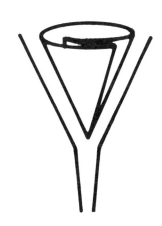

3 Collect the rock salt.

4 Crush the rock salt.

continued ➤

➤ *continued*

5. **Add water to the crushed rock salt.**

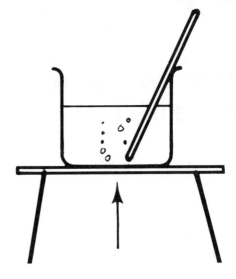

6. **Filter the mixture in the beaker.**

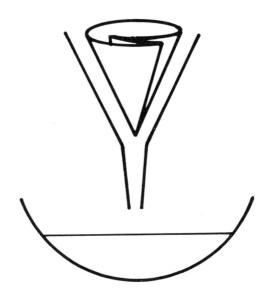

7. **Take the evaporating dish half full of liquid and heat it.**

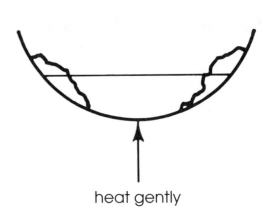

heat gently

Take care.
The salt as it forms can spit.

continued ➤

➤ continued

8 After cooling, the salt can be placed in a beaker as shown.

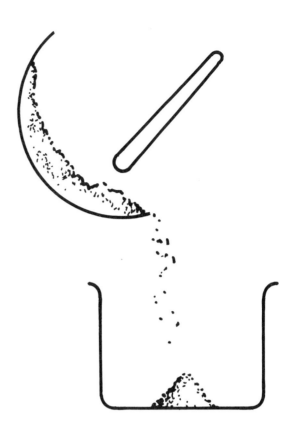

Did you manage to separate the sand and the salt?   Yes/no

Practical marks

Safety   _____

Doing the practical   _____

Following instructions _____

Completing the task   _____

Distillation

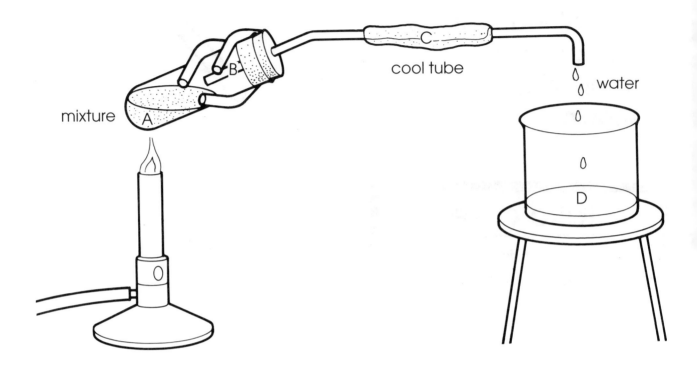

Here is a picture of a distillation system, where salt and water are separated. Circle the correct answer.

Where is the mixture of salt and water found?	A B C D
At what point is pure water found?	A B C D
Where does the liquid change into a gas?	A B C D
Where does the gas change into a liquid?	A B C D
Where is the apparatus hottest?	A B C D
Where is the cooling tube?	A B C D

UNDERSTANDING SCIENCE BOOK 1 PAGE 52

Readabout

Marie Curie

Read page 52.

Name: _____
Place of birth: _____
Year of birth: _____
Three interesting facts:
_____
_____
_____

Crossword

1 She won two Nobel prizes.
2 Hot, dry area with lots of sand.
3 Used to clean dirty water.
4 Does not dissolve in water.
5 This chemical kills cancer cells.

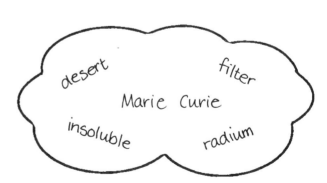

desert   filter   Marie Curie   insoluble   radium

Now ask to do skill sheets 13, 23.

UNDERSTANDING SCIENCE BOOK 1 PAGES 40-52

Unit 3 test

Name _____   Form _____

1 Which word best describes the changes shown in the pictures?

condensation   melting   evaporation   freezing

a

Ice turning into water is called

_____

b

Water appearing on a window is called

_____

c

Soup drying on a cooker is called

_____

2a Which clothes dry the fastest?

 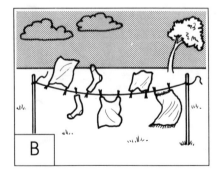 

Answer _____

➤ continued

72   US 1 Support Material

UNDERSTANDING SCIENCE BOOK 1 PAGES 40-52

➤ continued

3 Give two reasons why hairdriers are so quick at drying your hair.

Reason 1 _____

_____

Reason 2 _____

_____

4 Which sugar will dissolve the fastest?

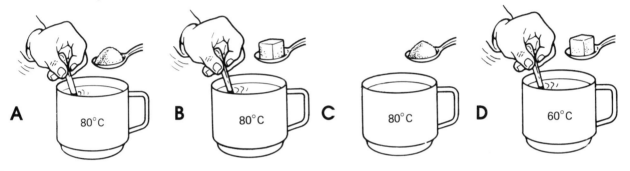

Answer _____

5 Name the following ways of separating mixtures.

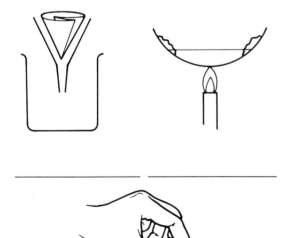

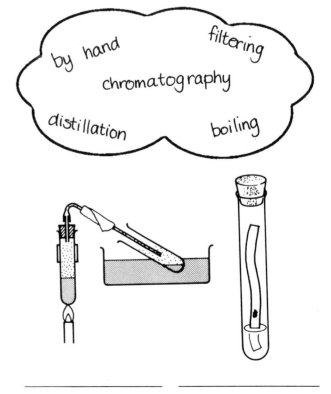

continued ➤

UNDERSTANDING SCIENCE BOOK 1 PAGES 40–52

➤ continued

6 Complete the following sentences.

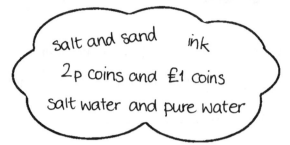

salt and sand   ink
2p coins and £1 coins
salt water and pure water

  a Filtering is used to separate
  _____

  b Chromatography is used to separate
  _____

  c Distillation is used to separate
  _____

  d You can separate _____
  by picking them up with your hands.

7 Look at the pictures below. Put them in the correct order, starting with C.

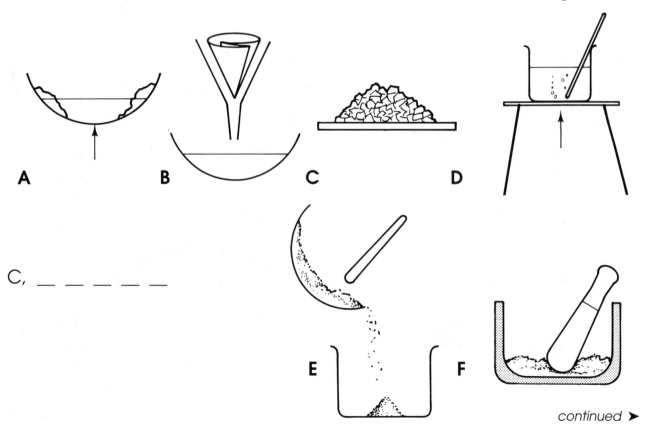

C, _ _ _ _ _

continued ➤

74   US 1 Support Material

UNDERSTANDING SCIENCE BOOK 1 PAGES 40-52

➤ continued

8 Look at the picture below. Label it.

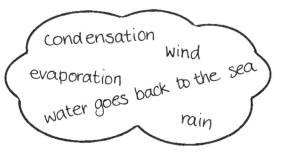
condensation
wind
evaporation
water goes back to the sea
rain

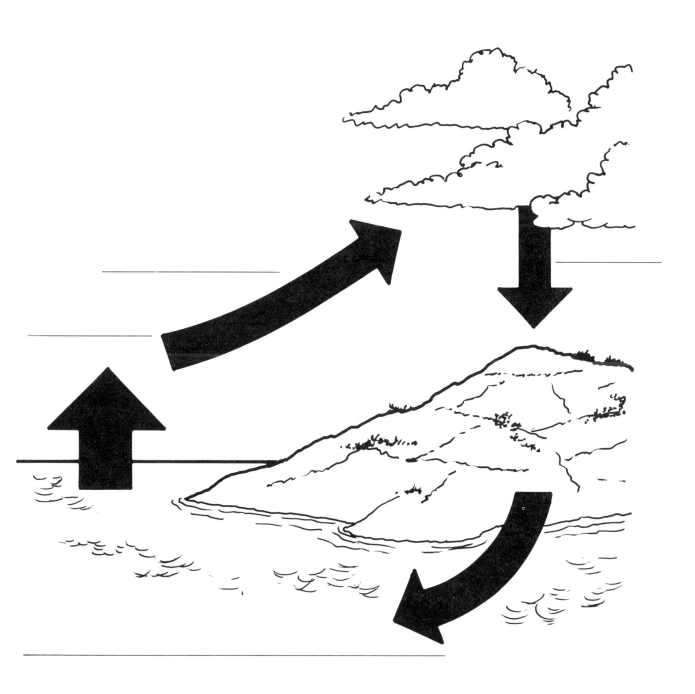

Forms of energy

energy	electrical	experiment
stored	forms	heat
movement	types	light
battery	wires	sound
bulb	hidden	

Complete the word search using the words above.

d	e	n	e	r	g	y	a	b	f	o	r	m	s	c	d
n	l	m	l	k	j	i	h	g	d	n	u	o	s	e	f
h	e	a	t	e	x	p	e	r	i	m	e	n	t	a	b
p	c	q	r	n	s	h	t	u	v	o	w	x	o	y	z
c	t	d	e	e	w	i	r	e	s	v	f	g	r	h	i
t	r	s	r	r	q	d	p	o	n	e	m	l	e	k	j
u	i	v	w	g	x	d	b	y	z	m	a	b	d	c	d
a	c	b	c	y	d	e	u	f	g	e	e	f	g	h	i
i	a	h	j	k	l	n	l	m	n	n	j	k	l	m	n
o	l	i	g	h	t	p	b	a	t	t	e	r	y	o	p
q	r	s	t	y	p	e	s	u	v	w	x	y	z	a	b
c	d	e	f	g	h	i	j	k	l	m	n	o	p	q	r

UNDERSTANDING SCIENCE BOOK 1 PAGES 54–55

The following words have been put back to front. Write them the correct way.

ygrene	
taeh	
thgil	
dnuos	
lacirtcele	
derots	
tnemevom	
yrettab	
blub	
tnemirepxe	

From the words above fill in the blanks.

e _ _ _ _ y

h _ _ _

s o _ _ _

e l _ _ _ _ _ _ a l

b a t _ _ _ _

UNDERSTANDING SCIENCE BOOK 1 PAGE 54

Energy in action

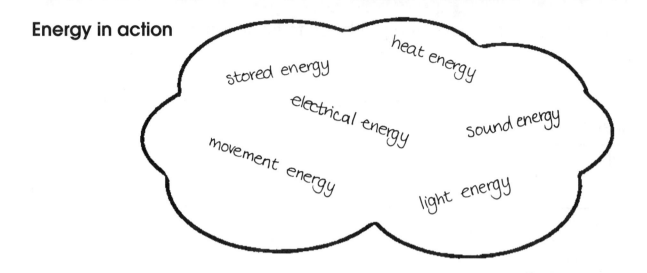

What form of energy do each of the following have?

_____   _____

_____   _____

_____   _____

Write a report of your experiment.

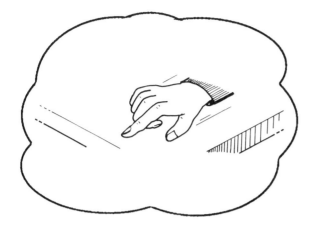
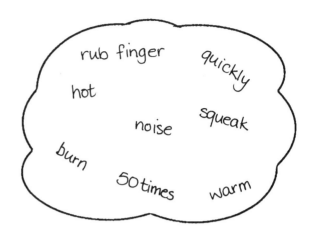

Diagram

Method

Results

UNDERSTANDING SCIENCE BOOK 1 PAGE 54

Write a report of your experiment.

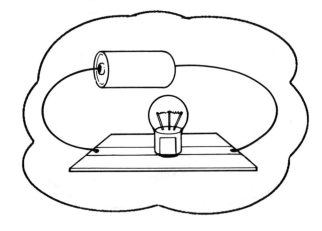 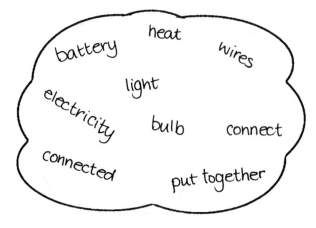

Diagram

Method
_____
_____
_____

Results
_____
_____
_____
_____

Energy in hiding

Write down the main forms of energy shown in the pictures.

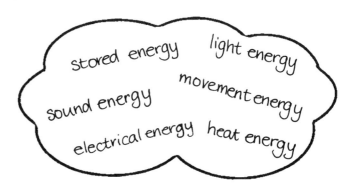
stored energy   light energy
sound energy   movement energy
electrical energy   heat energy

a Windmill turning
_____

f Mains socket
_____

b Breaking cup
_____

g Fire
_____

c Electric bulb
_____

h Food
_____

d Loudspeaker
_____

i Ice skater
_____

e Object up high
_____

j Sun
_____

Changing the form

UNDERSTANDING SCIENCE BOOK 1 PAGES 56–57

stored energy	movement	sound
light	heat	starting energy
bulb	experiment	finishing energy
hidden	bunsen burner	electrical

Complete the word search using the words above.

s	t	o	r	e	d	e	n	e	r	g	y	b	m
f	s	a	r	a	a	n	y	s	u	e	b	c	o
i	a	c	p	a	h	e	a	t	j	u	f	d	v
n	b	d	q	b	h	r	z	a	k	v	g	e	e
i	c	e	r	c	i	g	a	r	l	w	h	f	m
s	d	f	s	d	j	y	b	t	m	x	i	g	e
h	e	e	l	e	c	t	r	i	c	a	l	h	n
i	f	g	t	e	k	r	c	n	n	y	j	i	t
n	b	a	t	t	e	r	y	g	e	n	e	j	e
g	u	h	u	l	l	s	d	e	o	z	k	k	x
e	l	i	h	i	d	d	e	n	p	g	l	l	p
n	b	j	v	g	m	t	e	e	q	b	m	m	e
e	g	k	w	h	n	u	f	r	r	c	n	n	r
r	h	l	x	t	o	v	g	g	s	d	o	o	i
g	i	m	y	f	p	w	h	y	t	e	p	p	m
y	b	u	n	s	e	n	b	u	r	n	e	r	e
j	j	n	s	o	u	n	d	y	w	u	t	q	n
l	k	o	z	g	q	x	i	z	x	v	s	r	t

UNDERSTANDING SCIENCE BOOK 1 PAGES 56-57

The following words have been put back to front. Write them the correct way.

ygrene	
tnemevom	
dnuos	
gnitrats	
tnemirepxe	
neddih	
thgil	
derots	
lacirtcele	

From the words above fill in the blanks.

s _ _ _ _ _

l _ _ _ _

e l _ _ _ _ _ _ _ _

h _ _ _ _ _

e n _ _ _ _

UNDERSTANDING SCIENCE BOOK 1 PAGE 56

Energy for a change

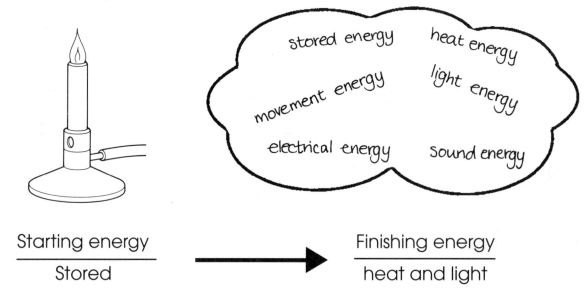

Starting energy: Stored ⟶ Finishing energy: heat and light

Complete the table.

Picture	Starting energy	Finishing energy
spiral / thread / heater		
yo-yo		
music box		
guitar		
duck		

continued ▶

UNDERSTANDING SCIENCE BOOK 1 PAGE 57

➤ *continued*

Picture	Starting energy	Finishing energy

US 1 Support Material

The machine scene

UNDERSTANDING SCIENCE BOOK 1 PAGES 58–61

machine	throat	kilojoules
fuel	muscles	calories
pressure	thermometer	brain
safety valve	peanut	steam

Complete the word search using the words above.

a	k	i	l	o	j	o	u	l	e	s	b	e	g
c	d	f	u	e	l	f	h	k	n	m	o	p	l
i	j	p	t	h	e	r	m	o	m	e	t	e	r
n	o	x	h	e	y	e	a	q	u	h	f	a	s
s	e	i	r	o	l	a	c	r	s	e	i	n	t
v	u	d	o	w	s	t	h	b	c	y	l	u	e
o	b	r	a	i	n	c	i	m	l	a	g	t	a
u	x	u	t	r	q	d	n	s	e	b	t	c	m
v	y	p	z	s	p	r	e	s	s	u	r	e	z
s	a	f	e	t	y	v	a	l	v	e	g	f	e

UNDERSTANDING SCIENCE BOOK 1 PAGES 58–61

The following words have been put back to front. Write them the correct way.

selcsum	
tunaep	
seirolac	
enihcam	
erusserp	
retemomreth	
seluojolik	
taorht	

From the words above fill in the blanks.

c a _ _ _ _ _ _

m u _ _ _ _ _

m _ _ h _ _ _

k _ _ _ j _ _ _ _ _

t h _ _ _ _ m _ _ _ _

UNDERSTANDING SCIENCE BOOK 1 PAGE 59

Big machines

Here is a diagram of a steam engine. Look at page 59 and label the diagram.

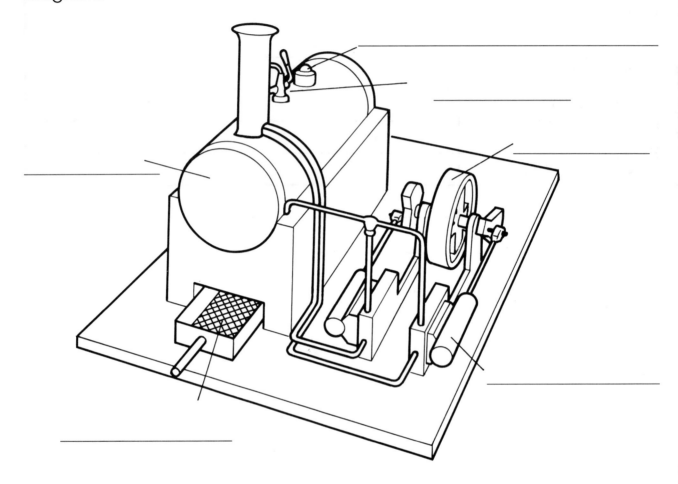

What happens in each of the following parts of the machine?

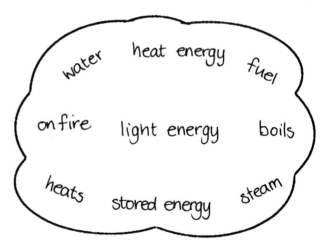

1 Fuel tray.

_____

_____

2 In the boiler.

_____

_____

UNDERSTANDING SCIENCE BOOK 1 PAGE 59

3 Why do we have a valve?

_____

_____

4 What happens to the pistons once we have steam?

_____

> safety valve   let out pressure
> steam   movement
> stored energy
> they move   light   heat energy

5 Give the energy changes in the following.

Name	Starting energy	Finishing energy
fuel burning		
water in the boiler		
steam moving the piston		

US 1 Support Material

Body machine

Complete the following by writing down the type of energy used.

Word bank: stored, movement, sound, heat energy, light, electrical

Noisy throat _____

Powerful muscle _____

Thoughtful energy. _____

Tubby tummy _____

Sweaty body _____

Energy form	Where it is produced in the body
sound	
movement	
stored	
light	
heat	
electrical	

Word bank: throat, nowhere, brain, fat, warm areas, muscles

Write a report of your experiment.

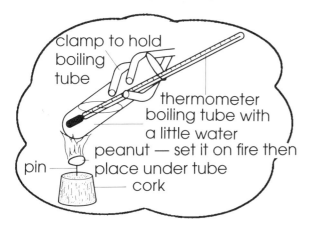
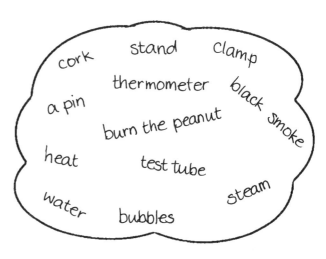

Diagram

Method

_____
_____
_____

Results

_____
_____
_____
_____

Temperature of water		
At beginning	At the end	Difference in temperature
°C	°C	°C

Energy from food

Energy in food is measured in kilojoules or in calories.

Average helping of	Kilojoules	Average helping of	Kilojoules	Average helping of	Kilojoules
apple	210	cucumber	20	potatoes	380
apple pie	840	custard	630	porridge	630
baked beans	1470	fish finger	210	rice	500
banana	300	grapefruit	120	rice pudding	720
beef curry	1260	haddock	500	sausage roll	1680
brussel sprouts	80	ice cream	500	scrambled egg	500
carrots	80	jam/marmalade	380	slice of bread	420
cheddar cheese	920	jelly	300	spaghetti	420
chicken	840	lemonade	760	tea, milk, sugar	210
chips	1130	lettuce	20	thick veg soup	630
cornflakes	420	milk	630	tomato	40
cottage cheese	120	pat of butter	210	yoghurt	590
cream soup	840	peas	80		
crisps	530	pizza	1260		

How much energy is there in the following foods?

Name	Energy kJ
chicken	8 4 0
apple	_ _ _
chips	_ _ _ _
crisps	_ _ _
ice cream	_ _ _
sausage roll	_ _ _ _
pizza	_ _ _ _

continued ▶

UNDERSTANDING SCIENCE BOOK 1 PAGE 61

➤ *continued*

Work out how much energy there is in eating the following.

Name	Energy value (kJ)
cream soup	
sausage roll	
baked beans	
chips	
ice cream	
	Total

Name	Energy value (kJ)
grapefruit	
cottage cheese	
lettuce	
cucumber	
tomato	
apple	
	Total

Write down the names of everything you eat at lunch time.

Name	Energy value (kJ)
	Total

UNDERSTANDING SCIENCE BOOK 1 PAGE 64

Readabout

Albert Einstein

Read page 64.

Name: _____
Place of birth: _____
Year of birth: _____
Three interesting facts:
_____
_____
_____

Crossword

1 Made in a power station.
2 Albert's surname.
3 Our bodies get energy from this.
4 Unit of energy in food like calories.
5 A steam engine is an example of one of these.

Einstein   electricity   machine   food   kilojoule

Now ask to do skill sheet 16.

UNDERSTANDING SCIENCE BOOK 1 PAGES 54–64

Unit 4 test

Name _____ Form _____

1 Write one sentence that describes the energy change in each picture. (The first one has been done for you.)

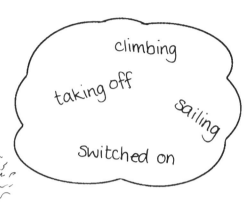
climbing
taking off
sailing
switched on

a The boat is moving in the current.

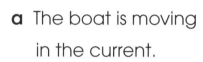

b The man is _____   c The ship is _____

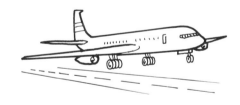

d The aeroplane is _____   e The TV is _____

2 Underline the six forms of energy below.

light	electricity	heat
gas	coal	movement
waves	sound	wind
tide	wood	stored
oil	sun	food

UNDERSTANDING SCIENCE BOOK 1 PAGES 54–64

➤ *continued*

3 Which energy form is present:

 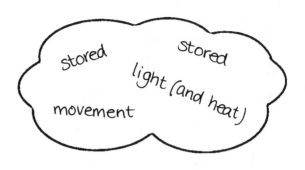

   a in a moving sledge? _____

   b in a balloon before it bursts?
   c in these?
   d in a light bulb which is on?

_____   _____   _____

4 At least four energy changes happen in a working steam engine. What is the finishing energy in each of the energy changes below?

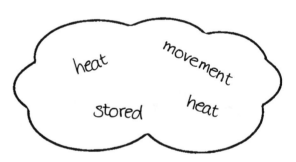

   a In the wheel: Movement → _____

   b Burning the fuel: Stored → _____

   c In the piston: Stored → _____

   d In the boiler: Heat → _____

First measurements

balance	length	measuring cylinder
mass	centimetres	volume
weight	degree	cubic centimetres
grams	time	thermometer
ruler	seconds	temperature

Complete the word search using the words above.

```
s c d e g r e e a n b e f u n b u t s
c e n t i m e t r e s e w i t h a p e
s a f e t y i n m i n d a l l h e t i
a b c w e i g h t d t e f g h i j k l
m v n o p q r s i t h u v w x y z a b
c o d e f g h i m j e k l m n o p q r
s l e n g t h e u r u l e r v w x y
c u b i c c e n t i m e t r e s k l m
a m b c l d e s e c o n d s f g h i j
n e o p o q r s t e m p e r a t u r e
t u v w c x y z a b e c s d e f g h i
j k l m k n o p q r t s s t u v w x y
b a l a n c e j k l e m a n o p q r s
a b c d e f g h i g r a m s t u v w x
m e a s u r i n g c y l i n d e r y z
```

UNDERSTANDING SCIENCE BOOK 1 PAGES 66-74

The following words have been put back to front. Write them the correct way.

emit	
relur	
ssam	
erutarepmet	
smarg	
htgnel	
emulov	
ecnalab	
eerged	

From the words above fill in the blanks.

b _ _ _ _ _ _

m _ _ _

r _ _ _ _

t _ _ _

d _ _ _ _ _

Measurement scales

Name the following instruments.

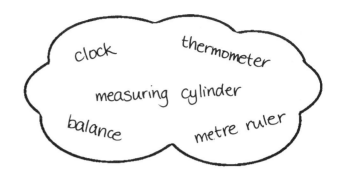

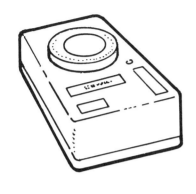

_____

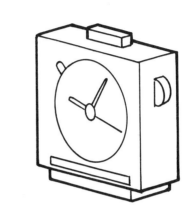

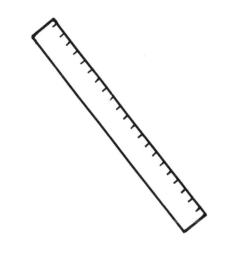

_____

_____

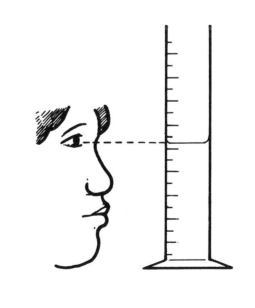

_____

_____

UNDERSTANDING SCIENCE BOOK 1 PAGE 66

1 Tick the correct word.

A clock is used to measure

weight _____   length _____   time _____   temperature _____

A measuring cylinder is used to measure

weight _____   volume _____   time _____   length _____

A thermometer is used to measure

volume _____   time _____   length _____   temperature _____

A balance is used to measure

mass _____   time _____   length _____   temperature _____

2 Match the units to the instruments.

clock   centimetres

ruler   seconds

thermometer   celsius

Measurement puzzle 1

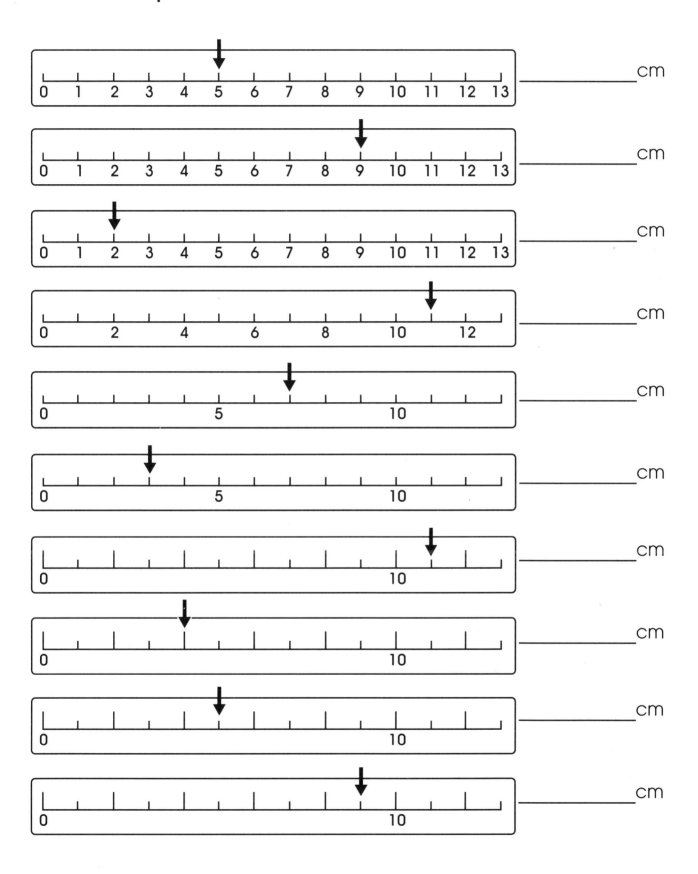

continued ➤

UNDERSTANDING SCIENCE BOOK 1 PAGE 67

➤ *continued*

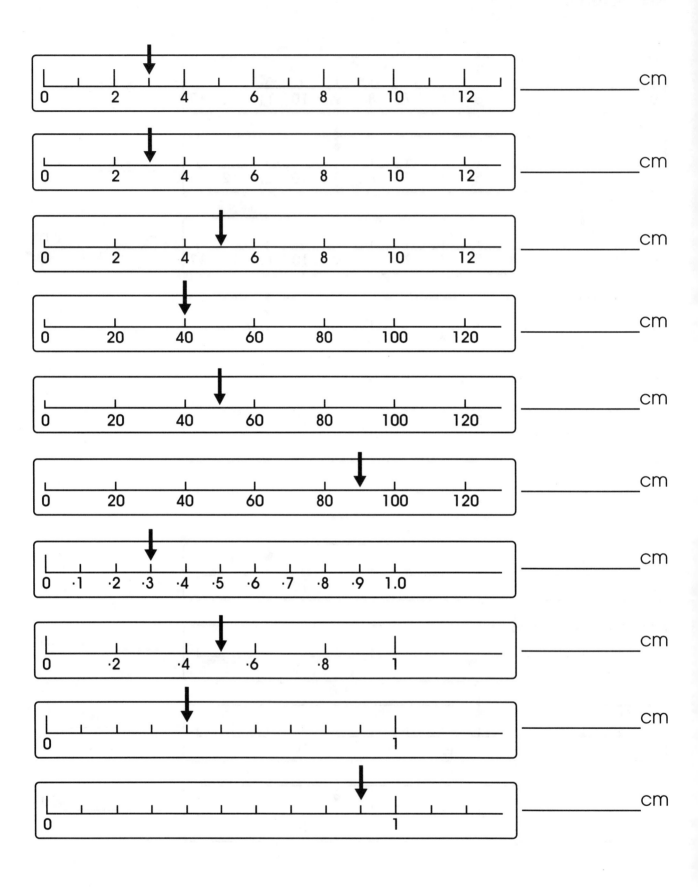

Measurement puzzle 2

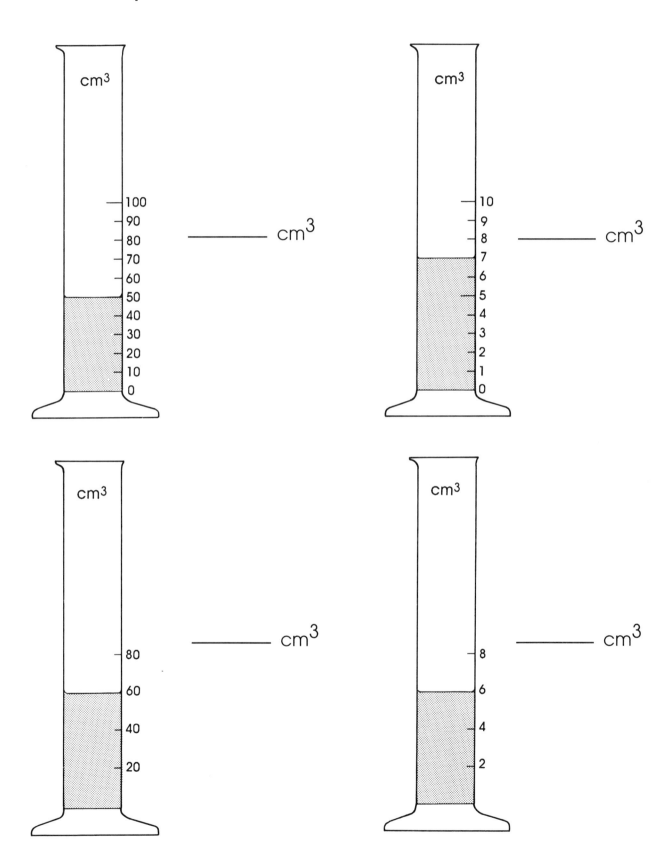

continued ➤

➤ *continued*

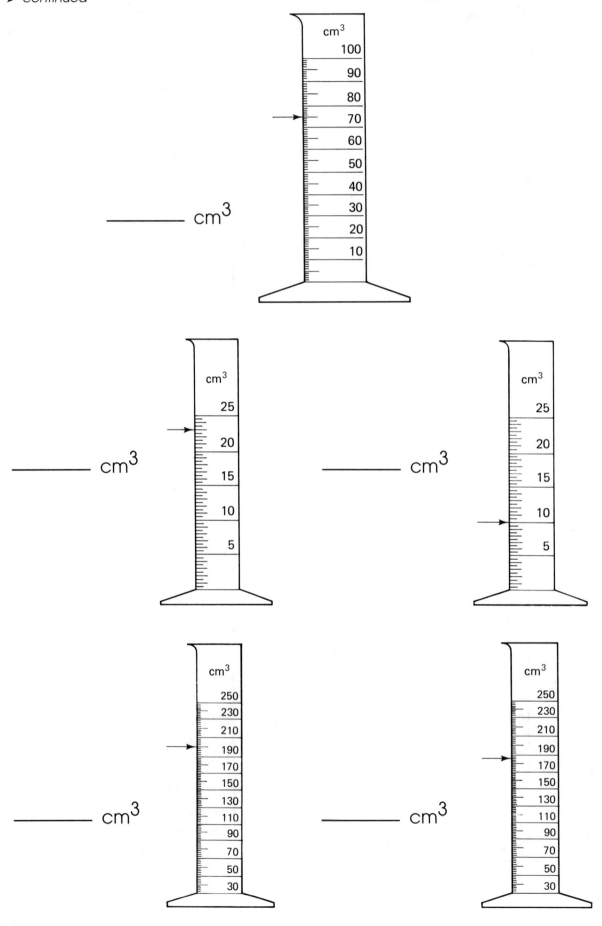

Measurement puzzle 3

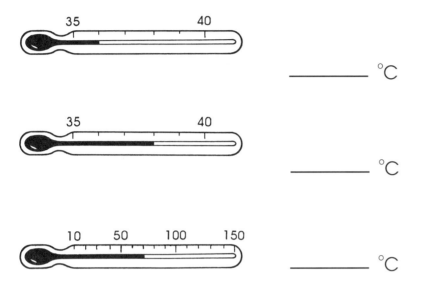

_____ °C

_____ °C

_____ °C

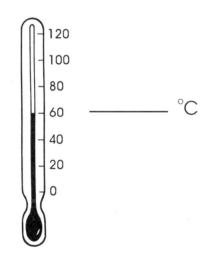 _____ °C

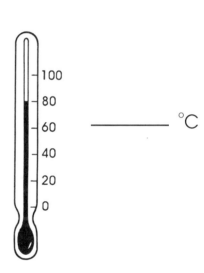 _____ °C

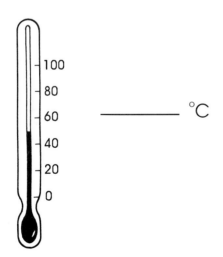 _____ °C

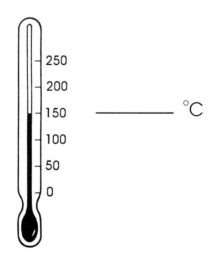 _____ °C

continued ➤

➤ *continued*

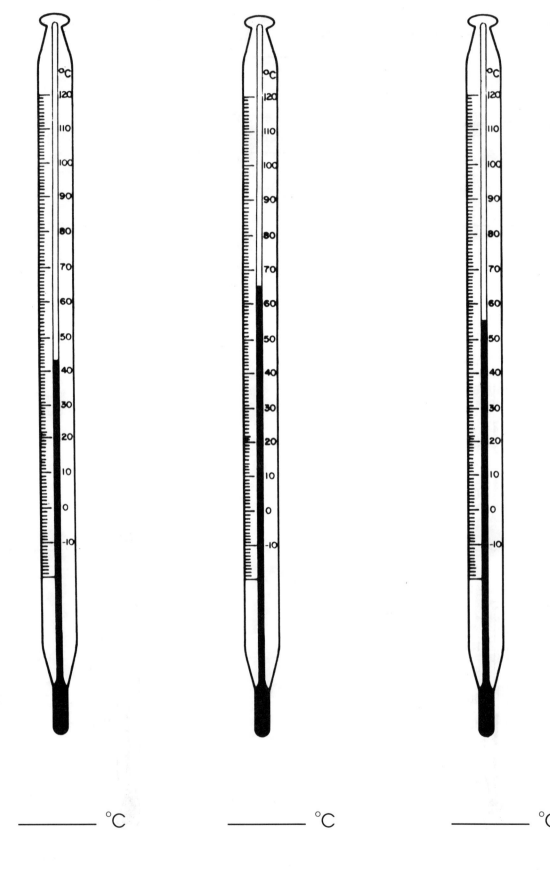

_____ °C   _____ °C   _____ °C

UNDERSTANDING SCIENCE BOOK 1 PAGE 67

Measurement puzzle 4

Write each of the following against the correct temperature.

ice   boiling water   room temperature   body temperature

- 100°C _____

- 37°C   _____

- 20°C   _____

- 0°C   _____

US 1 Support Material

Measurement puzzle 5

What is the reading at each arrow?

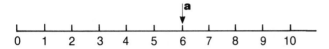

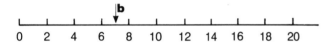

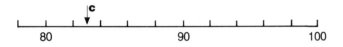

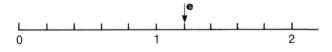

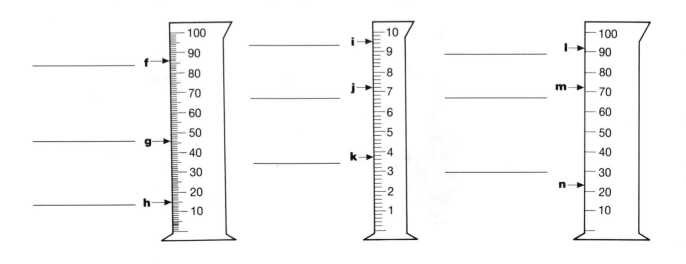

Measurement puzzle 6

Make and record the following measurements using the correct modern instruments.

a Mass of a milk bottle   balance   **b** Height of your seat   ruler

 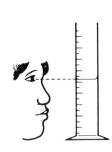 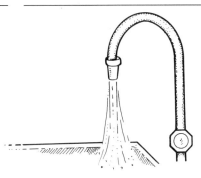 

c Volume of a carton   measuring cylinder   **d** Temperature of tap water   thermometer

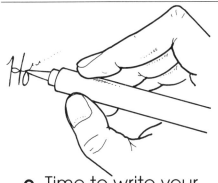 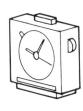

e Time to write your name five times   stop watch

UNDERSTANDING SCIENCE BOOK 1 PAGE 71

Reading graphs

Copy the bar graph that is on page 71.

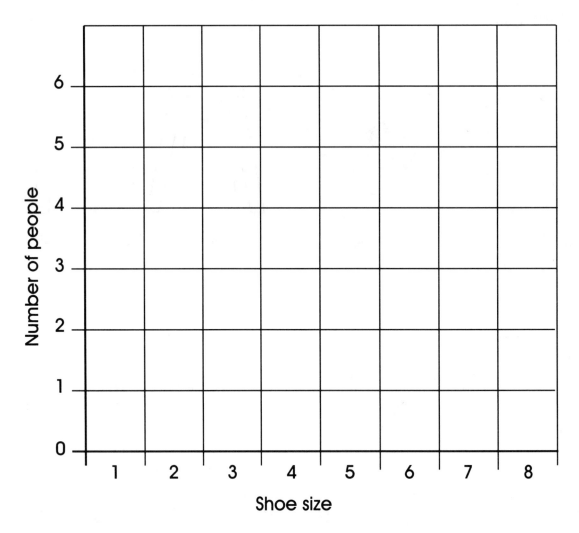

1 What is the most common shoe size? _____

2 What is the least common shoe size? _____

3 How many people have size 6 shoes? _____

4 What is the biggest shoe size in this group? _____

5 How many people had their shoe size measured? _____

UNDERSTANDING SCIENCE BOOK 1 PAGE 71

Pie chart

Look at the pie chart on page 71. Complete the copy of the pie chart below by putting in the following numbers.

43   3   9   45

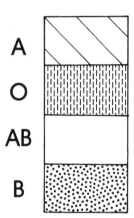
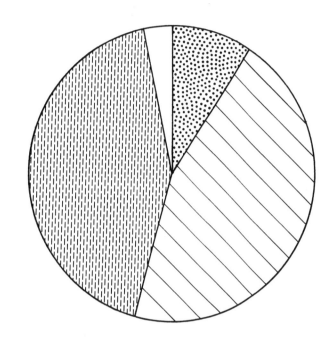

Colour the pie chart using the key to find out the correct colours.

1 How many blood groups are there? _____

2 What is the most common blood group? _____

3 What is the least common blood group? _____

4 How many people have blood group A? _____

5 How many people had their blood group tested? _____

US 1 Support Material

Readabout

Aristotle

Read page 74.

Name: _____
Place of birth: _____
Year of birth: _____
Three interesting facts:
_____
_____
_____

Crossword

1 Unit of mass.
2 Country where Aristotle was born.
3 We use a clock to measure this.
4 Length is measured using one of these.
5 Thermometers are used to measure this.

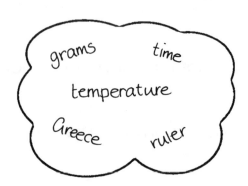

grams   time   temperature   Greece   ruler

Now ask to do skill sheets 27, 29, 30, 33, 34, 35, 36, 38, 39, 43, 44.

UNDERSTANDING SCIENCE BOOK 1 PAGES 66–74

Unit 5 test

Name _____   Form _____

1 Name the following.

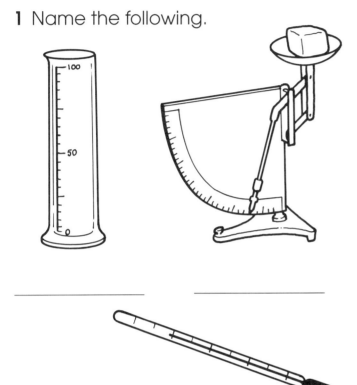

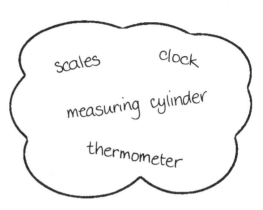
scales   clock   measuring cylinder   thermometer

2 Give the correct temperature for each of the following.

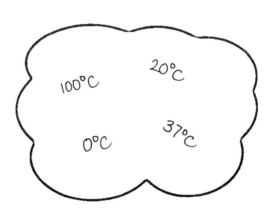
100°C   20°C   0°C   37°C

   a Melting ice _____ °C

   b Boiling water _____ °C

   c Your body temperature ____ °C

   d A classroom in the summer _____ °C

continued ➤

US 1 Support Material

UNDERSTANDING SCIENCE BOOK 1 PAGES 66–74

➤ continued

3 Give the name of the instrument used to measure:

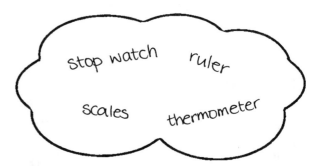

a time _____

b temperature _____

c your height _____   **d** your weight _____

4 Give the values of the following.

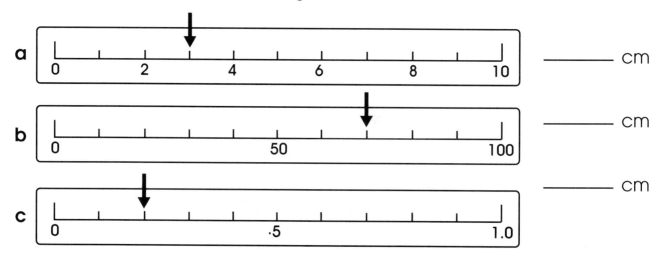

a _____ cm

b _____ cm

c _____ cm

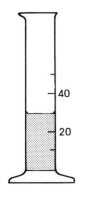

_____ cm³

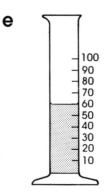

_____ cm³

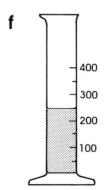

_____ cm³

continued ➤

UNDERSTANDING SCIENCE BOOK 1 PAGES 66–74

➤ *continued*

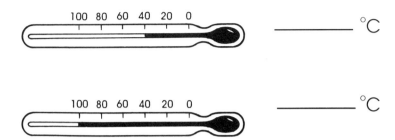

_____ °C

_____ °C

5 Here are the results for the games played by pupils in form seven.

Girls			Boys		
Sport	**Tally**	**Total**	**Sport**	**Tally**	**Total**
football	III	3	football	̶H̶I̶I̶ III	
rugby	II	2	rugby	IIII	
hockey	̶H̶I̶I̶ ̶H̶I̶I̶ ̶H̶I̶I̶	15	hockey	̶H̶I̶I̶	
basketball	̶H̶I̶I̶ ̶H̶I̶I̶	10	basketball	̶H̶I̶I̶ ̶H̶I̶I̶ III	
total		30			

a Complete the total for boys in each sport. The girls' values are done for you.

b Put the values for the boys on a bar chart.

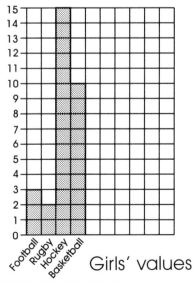

Girls' values

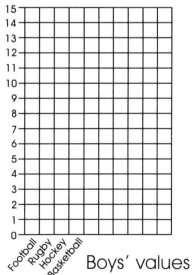

Boys' values

continued ➤

6 The dinner ladies asked pupils which meal they enjoyed the most. The results are shown below.

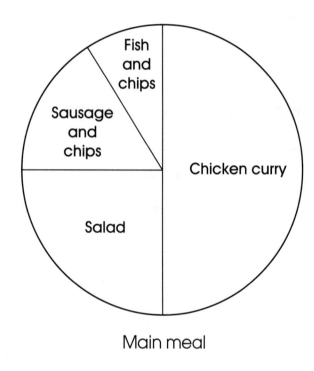

Main meal   Pudding

a Which main meal was most popular? _____

b Which main meal was least popular? _____

c What would you have chosen? _____

d Which pudding was favourite? _____

e How many pupils eat cake and custard? _____

f Which pudding was least popular? _____

UNDERSTANDING SCIENCE BOOK 1 PAGES 76-77

Electric problems 1

electricity	socket	problems
electric	power pack	bright
light	battery	repair
difficulty	circuit	design
dangerous	symbol	ideas

Complete the word search using the words above.

```
d i f f i c u l t y r e t t a b r
e a b c d e f i g h i j k l m n e
s o p q r e s g t u v w x y z a p
i d e a s l b h c d e f g s h i a
g s j e l e c t r i c i t y k l i
n m m n o c i r c u i t p m q r r
s e t u v t w x y z a b c b d e f
g l j m o r q r s t u v w o x y z
n b k b r i g h t s l o r l w z c
i o l n p c g h j o m p s u x a d
a r b c d e f i k c n q t v x b e
a p o w e r p a c k b c d e f g h
i j k l m n o p q e r s t u v w x
y z a b c d e f g t h i j k l m n
o d a n g e r o u s p q r s t u v
```

US 1 Support Material

117

UNDERSTANDING SCIENCE BOOK 1 PAGES 76–77

The following words have been put back to front. Write them the correct way.

thgil	
lobmys	
tekcos	
tiucric	
cirtcele	
yrettab	
rewop	
thgirb	
ngised	
saedi	

From the words above fill in the blanks.

e _ _ _ _ _ i c

l _ _ _ _

s _ _ _ _ t

c _ _ _ _ _ t

s y _ _ _ _

Symbols

Give the symbol for a battery.

Give the symbol for a bulb.

Give the symbol for a wire.

Make a complete circuit with a battery, bulb and wires.

UNDERSTANDING SCIENCE BOOK 1 PAGE 77

Solve the problem

Explain how each of the problems below can be sorted out.

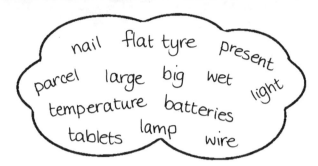

nail flat tyre present
parcel large big wet light
temperature batteries
tablets lamp wire

continued ➤

UNDERSTANDING SCIENCE BOOK 1 PAGE 77

➤ *continued*

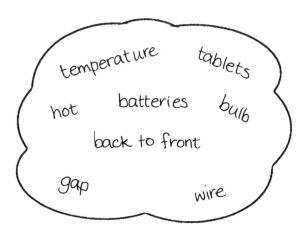

_____
_____
_____

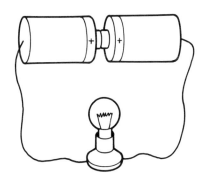

_____
_____
_____

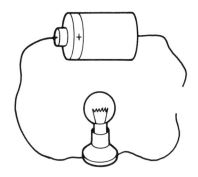

_____
_____
_____

US 1 Support Material

UNDERSTANDING SCIENCE BOOK 1 PAGES 78-83

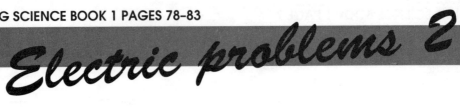

series	material	resistance
parallel	conductor	plastic
bulb	insulator	metal
circuit	batteries	experiment
dimmer	electricity	light

Complete the word search using the words above.

```
c o n d u c t o r a b c d e f e g
h i j k l d m n o p q r s t u l v
r w e x c i r c u i t y z a b e c
e d x e f m g h i j k l m n o c p
s q p r s m p l a s t i c t u t v
i w e x z e a b c d e b f g h r i
s j r k l r m m n o s u p q r i s
t t i u p a r a l l e v w x c y
a a m b c d e t f g r b h i j i k
n l e m n o p e q r i s t u v t w
c x n y z a b r c d e e f g h y i
e j t k l m n i i n s u l a t o r
o p m e t a l a q r s t u v w x y
l i g h t a b l e x p c r r m e n
a b c d e f g h i j k l m n o p q
b a t t e r i e s r s t u v w x y
```

UNDERSTANDING SCIENCE BOOK 1 PAGES 78-83

The following words have been put back to front. Write them the correct way.

seires	
tiucric	
blub	
lellarap	
remmid	
lairetam	
rotalusni	
rotcudnoc	
seirettab	

From the words above fill in the blanks.

s _ _ _ _ _

p _ _ _ _ _ e l

c _ _ _ u i t

d _ _ _ _ _

b _ _ _

Conductors and insulators

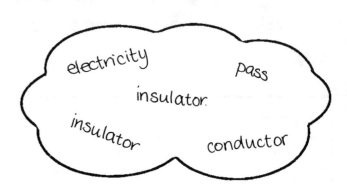

| conductors — pass electricity |
| insulators — do not pass electricity |

Fill in the gaps using the word puddle above.

A conductor allows e_____ to p_____ through it.

An i_____ does not allow electricity to pass through it.

Plastic is an example of an i _____

Metal is an example of a c _____

UNDERSTANDING SCIENCE BOOK 1 PAGE 78

Write a report of your experiment.

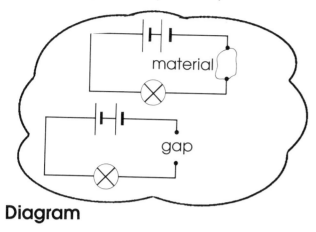
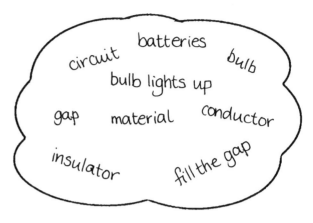

Diagram

Method

_____
_____
_____
_____

Results

Material	Conductor	Insulator
glass beaker		
1p piece		
iron nail		
rubber tubing		
wool		
aluminium window frame		
wooden ruler		

Write a report of your experiment.

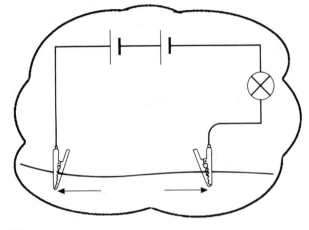
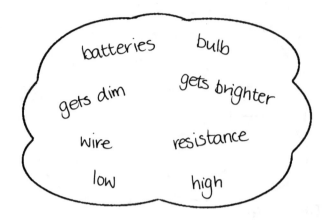

Diagram

Method

Results

Series and parallel

Which of the following are in series and which are in parallel?

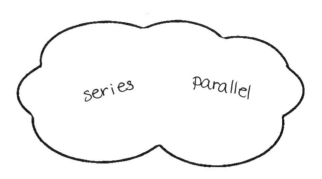

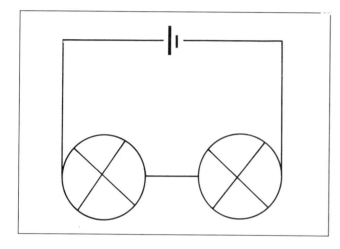

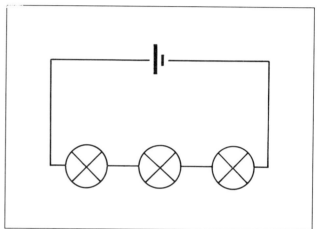

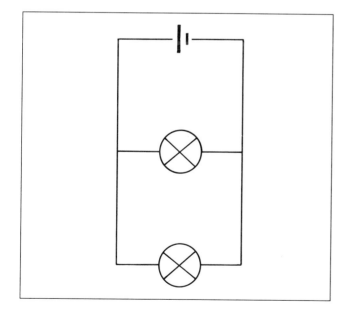

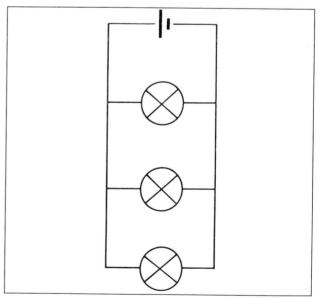

UNDERSTANDING SCIENCE BOOK 1 PAGE 82

House lighting

Circuit 1

series

Circuit 2

parallel

If a bulb was to blow in *circuit 1* would the rest work? _____

If a bulb was to blow in *circuit 2* would the rest work? _____

Which circuit would be the best to use in school buildings or a house?
_____

Why?
_____
_____
_____

UNDERSTANDING SCIENCE BOOK 1 PAGES 84–85

 Plugs

fuse	flex	wires
electric	live	screws
socket	neutral	flex grip
dangerous	earth	plastic cover
plug	three-core flex	terminals

Complete the word search using the words above.

```
t h r e e c o r e f l e x q e p o
e a b c d e f g s h i j k l l m n
r p l a s t i c c o v e r m e p q
m a b c d e f g r h i j k l c n o
i s t u v w x n e u t r a l t y z
n a b c d e f g w i r e s i r h i
a j k l m n o p s q r a s v l t u
l v w x y z a b c d e r f e c g h
s i j k l m n o p q r t s t u v w
f l e x g r i p l u g h x y z a b
l c d e f u s e j k l m n o p q r
e s t u v w x y z a b c d e f g h
x d a n g e r o u s o c k e t a b
c e l e c t r i c i t y d e f g h
i j k l m n o p q r s t u v w x y
a b c d e f g h i j k l m n o p q
h e l l o s c i e n c e i s f u n
```

US 1 Support Material 129

UNDERSTANDING SCIENCE BOOK 1 PAGES 84-85

The following words have been put back to front. Write them the correct way.

htrae	
xelf	
evil	
lartuen	
esuf	
suoregnad	
gulp	
tekcos	
swercs	
slanimret	

From the words above fill in the blanks.

e _ _ _ _

f _ _ x

l _ _ _

n _ _ _ _ _ _

f _ _ _

Wire a plug

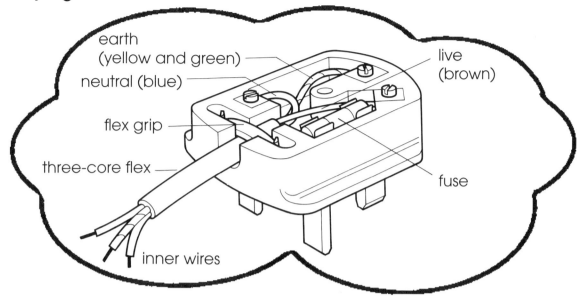

Label the diagram below.

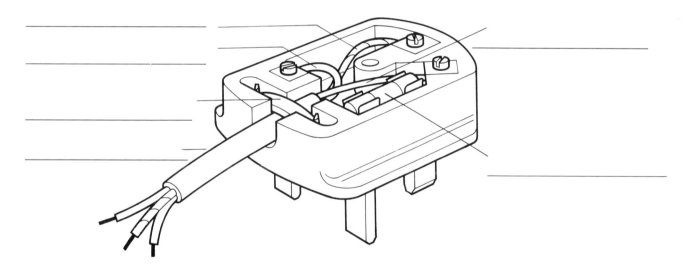

What are the colours of the following wires:

live   _____

earth   _____

neutral?   _____

UNDERSTANDING SCIENCE BOOK 1 PAGE 85

Making decisions

Explain what's wrong in each of the pictures below.

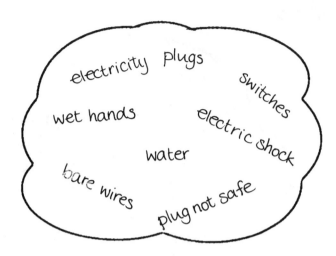

electricity plugs switches wet hands electric shock water bare wires plug not safe

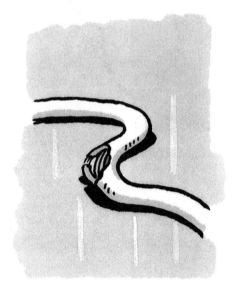

UNDERSTANDING SCIENCE BOOK 1 PAGES 86-87

Static electricity

static	spark	crackle
attract	comb	petrol
bacteria	lightning	trickle
operating	theatre	nylon

Complete the word search using the words above.

s	t	a	t	i	c	l	e	n	a	u
p	v	a	z	d	r	z	c	o	m	b
a	o	t	c	g	a	f	b	p	y	a
r	x	t	r	i	c	k	l	e	p	c
k	x	r	h	g	k	s	l	r	e	t
m	e	a	n	y	l	o	n	a	t	e
d	t	c	t	h	e	f	b	t	r	r
e	r	t	a	e	h	t	k	i	o	i
j	o	k	c	r	l	a	m	n	l	a
l	i	g	h	t	n	i	n	g	o	n

US 1 Support Material

UNDERSTANDING SCIENCE BOOK 1 PAGES 86-87

The following words have been put back to front. Write them the correct way.

citats	
tcartta	
ertaeht	
nolyn	
elkcarc	
gninthgil	
bmoc	
kraps	
elkcirt	

From the words above fill in the blanks.

n _ _ _ _

c _ _ _

s t _ _ _ _

c _ _ c _ _ _

l _ _ _ _ n _ _ _

UNDERSTANDING SCIENCE BOOK 1 PAGE 86

Static problems

What is happening below?

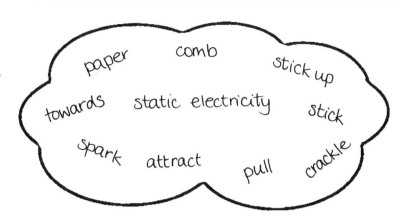

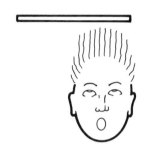 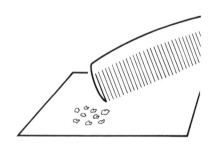 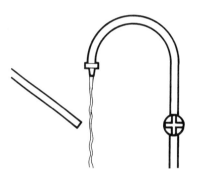

_____   _____   _____
_____   _____   _____
_____   _____   _____

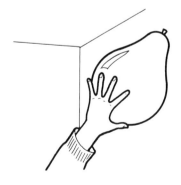  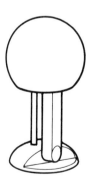

_____   _____   _____
_____   _____   _____
_____   _____   _____
_____   _____   _____

US 1 Support Material

UNDERSTANDING SCIENCE BOOK 1 PAGE 87

Static solutions

Look at page 87.

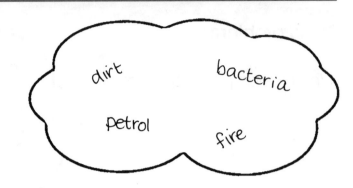

Fill in the missing words.

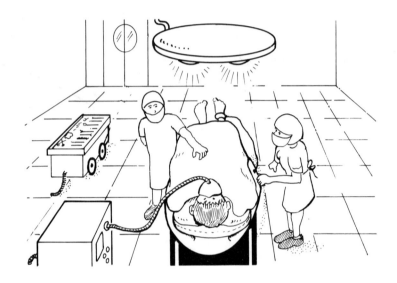

Static electricity in an operating theatre attracts _____ and _____

Static electricity at a petrol pump could set the _____ on _____

Readabout

Alessandro Volta

Read page 90.

Name: _____
Place of birth: _____
Year of birth: _____
Three interesting facts:
_____
_____
_____

Crossword

1 Used to work a radio. Does not need a plug.
2 Country where Volta was born.
3 Used for heating and lighting.
4 Steals your belongings.
5 Makes your hair stand up.

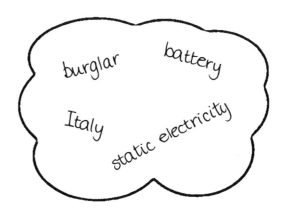

Now ask to do skill sheets

UNDERSTANDING SCIENCE BOOK 1 PAGES 76-90

Unit 6 test

Name _____ Form _____

1 Give the symbol for a:

battery   bulb   switch

2 Why don't the bulbs light up in the circuits below?

bulb   battery   batteries   wire

continued ➤

➤ *continued*

3 Which of the following are insulators and which are conductors?

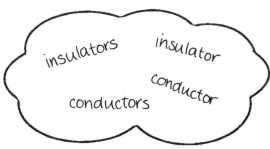
insulators   insulator   conductor   conductors

glass beaker	1p piece	iron nail

insulator		

rubber tubing	wool	wooden ruler

4 Look at the picture of the plug. Circle the correct answer.

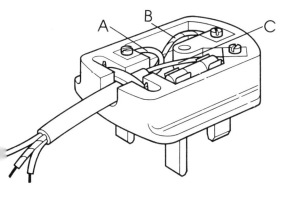

a Where is the live wire?   A   B   C
b Where is the earth wire?   A   B   C
c Where is the neutral wire?   A   B   C

continued ➤

UNDERSTANDING SCIENCE BOOK 1 PAGES 76-90

➤ continued

    d What colour is the live wire?

    _____

    e What colour is the earth wire?

    _____

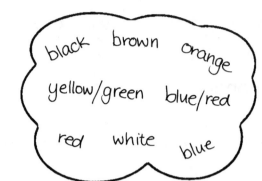

    f What colour is the neutral wire? _____

5 Which of the circuits below are in series and which are in parallel?

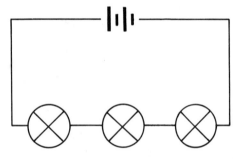 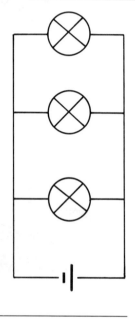

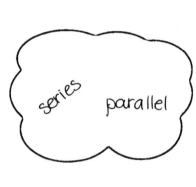

_____ _____

6 Which circuit has the brightest bulb, A, B or C?

    The answer is _____

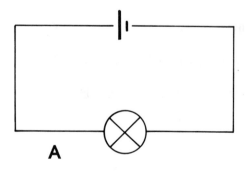 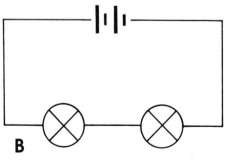 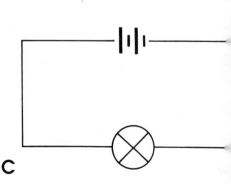

A   B   C

UNDERSTANDING SCIENCE BOOK 1 PAGES 92-93

Look small

microscope	scanning	slide
magnify	electron	mirror
magnifies	objective	eyepiece
appear	lens	focus
light microscope	stage	control

Complete the word search using the words above.

```
o b j e c t i v e a b c a d e f e g
h i j k l m n o p q r s p t u v y w
x y z a b c d e f g h i p j k l e m
n o p m i c r o s c o p e q r s p t
a b c a e d c l b a z y a x w v i u
d m a g n i f i e s m i r r o r e e
f l e n s g h g i c j k l m n o c p
q r s i t t u h v a w x y z a b e c
d e f f a g h t i n j f o c u s k l
m n o y g p q m r n s t u v w x y z
s l i d e a b i c i d e f g h i j k
l m n o p q r c s n t c o n t r o l
u v w x y z a r b g c d e f g h i j
k l m n o p q o r s t u v w x y z a
b e d e f g h s i j k l m n o p q r
s t u v w x y c z a b c d e f g h i
j k l m n o p o n q r s t u v w x y
a b c d e f g p e l e c t r o n g h
i j k l m n o e p q r s t u v w x y
```

US 1 Support Material

UNDERSTANDING SCIENCE BOOK 1 PAGES 92-93

The following words have been put back to front. Write them the correct way.

epocsorcim	
rorrim	
yfingam	
edils	
evitcejbo	
sucof	
lortnoc	
egats	
nortcele	
gninnacs	

From the words above fill in the blanks.

m i _ _ _ _ _ _ _ _

m a _ _ _ _ _

o _ _ _ _ _ i v e

f _ _ _ _

s _ _ _ _

Microscope parts

Look at page 92.

Label the diagram below.

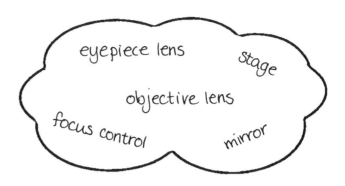

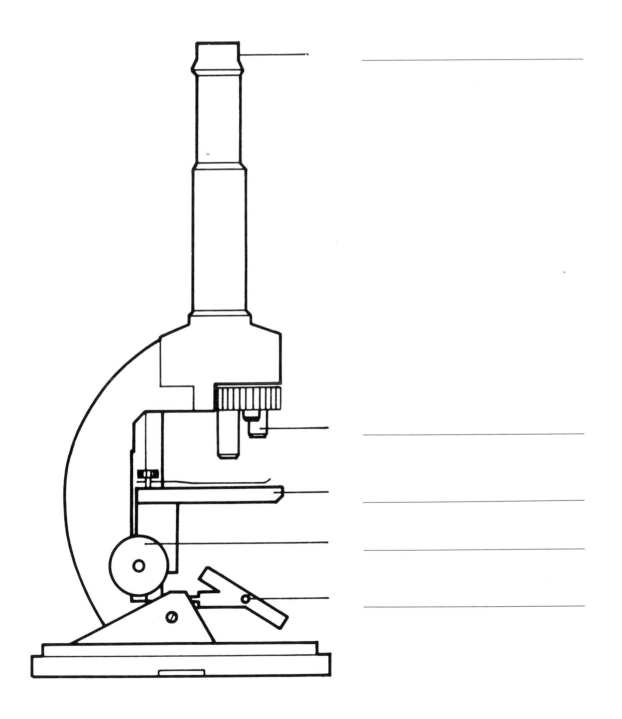

Look at a slide under the microscope.

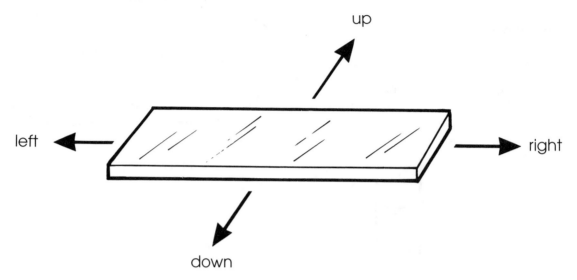

What happens under the microscope when you move the slide:

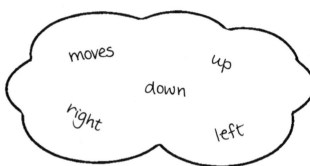

up _____

down _____

left _____

right? _____

UNDERSTANDING SCIENCE BOOK 1 PAGES 94-97

Building bricks

cell	cytoplasm	chloroplasts
membrane	chemical	food
controls	nucleus	sunlight
discovery	cell wall	vacuole
stain	shape	solution

Complete the word search using the words above.

```
s a m b c d v n u c l e u s e
o c e f g h a i j e k l m n o
l o m p q r c s f l t u v w x
u n b y z a u b o l c d e s f
t t r c h l o r o p l a s t s
i r a y g h l i d j k l u a m
o o n t c h e m i c a l n i u
n l e o c n o p q e r s l n t
v s x p l k l m n l a b i v w
a b c l l o p q r l c d g t u
a c d a s s t u v w e f h r s
e f g s w x y s h a p e t p q
h i j m a b c d e l f g h i j
d i s c o v e r y l k l m n o
```

US 1 Support Material

UNDERSTANDING SCIENCE BOOK 1 PAGES 94-97

The following words have been put back to front. Write them the correct way.

sllec	
enarbmem	
slortnoc	
yrevocsid	
niats	
epahs	
stsalporolhc	
suelcun	
msalpotyc	
eloucav	

From the words above fill in the blanks.

c y _ _ _ _ _ _ _

n _ _ _ _ _ _

s t _ _ _

c h _ _ _ _ _ _ _ _ _ _

v _ _ _ _ _ _

Write a report of your experiment.

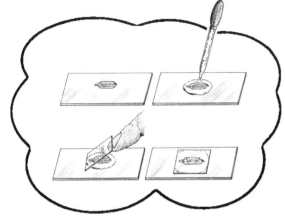
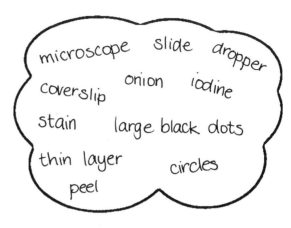

Diagram

Method

Results

Diagram of cells

Cells

Label each of the following diagrams.

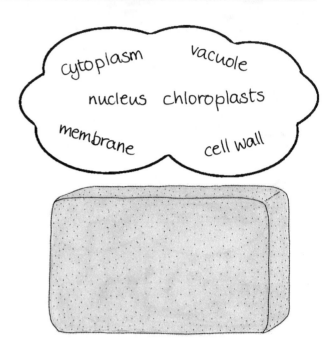
cytoplasm   vacuole   nucleus   chloroplasts   membrane   cell wall

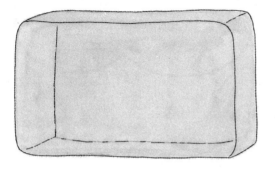

_____

_____

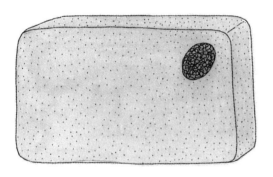

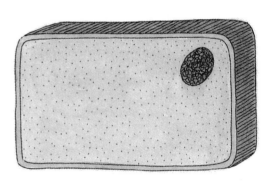

_____

_____

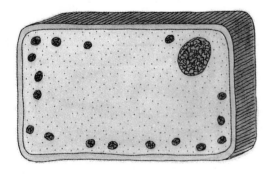

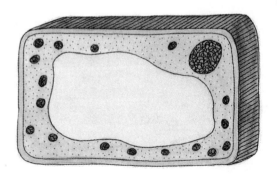

_____

_____

Parts of a cell

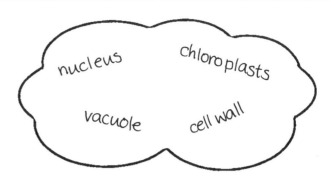

Complete the crossword.

1 This controls the cell.
2 This gives a plant cell its shape.
3 These are used by a plant cell to make food.
4 This holds liquid in a cell.

Cell types

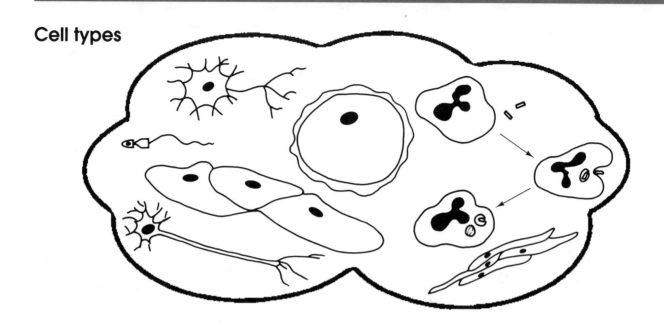

Draw a picture of each of the following cells.

Sex cell	Muscle cell
Brain cell	Motor nerve cell
White blood cell	Skin cell

UNDERSTANDING SCIENCE BOOK 1 PAGES 98–104

sex cell	stigma	seed
sperm	stamen	maturity
egg	pollination	female
ovary	fertilisation	male
pollen	dispersal	courtship

Complete the word search using the words above.

```
o v a r y a b c d p e m f c f
f g h i j k l m n o o a p o e
a d i s p e r s a l q t r u r
b s t s e x c e l l u u v r t
t w x p g y z e a e b r c t i
c d e e g f g d h n i i t s l
d a b r c d e s a b c t d h i
e a b m c d c t a b c y d i s
z f e m a l e a m d e c a p a
a a d s t i g m a f e a a b t
t b e b a c e e l b a d b e i
l c a c b d a n e c b e c d o
p o l l i n a t i o n a b c n
```

UNDERSTANDING SCIENCE BOOK 1 PAGES 98-104

The following words have been put back to front. Write them the correct way.

nellop	
amgits	
nemats	
noitasilitref	
ytirutam	
mreps	
yravo	
pihstruoc	
noitanillop	
lasrepsid	

From the words above fill in the blanks.

s _ _ g _ _

s _ a _ _ _

m _ _ _ _ _ _

p _ _ _ _ _ _ _ _

f _ _ _ _ _ _ _ _ _ _ _

Animal reproduction

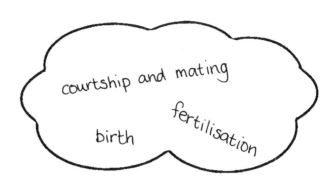

Ask for resource sheets 7.4A and E7.4. Fill them in.

Name the following.

The sperm enters the egg cell. This happens outside the female body in most fish and amphibians. It happens inside the body in reptiles, birds and mammals.	_____
The male and female meet. This is courtship. The male sperm is put near the female egg. This is mating.	_____
The baby animal is born. In many animals it hatches from an egg. In mammals it comes directly from the mother's body.	_____

UNDERSTANDING SCIENCE BOOK 1 PAGE 98

Put the following pictures in the correct order.
Begin with D.

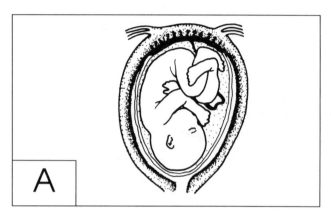
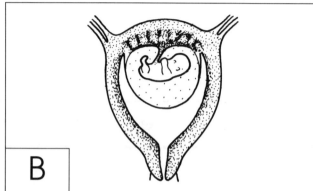
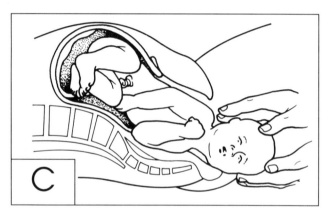
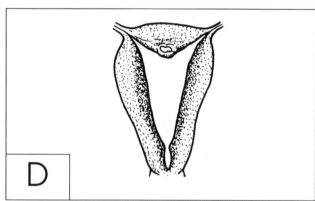
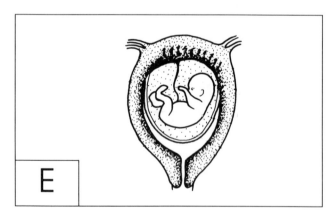
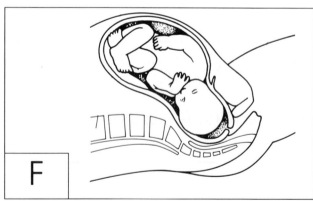

Give the correct order of the pictures.

D _ _ _ _ _

Plant reproduction

Look at page 100.

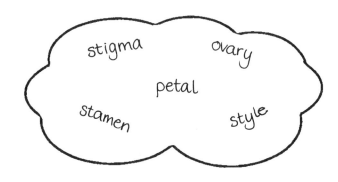

Label the diagram below.

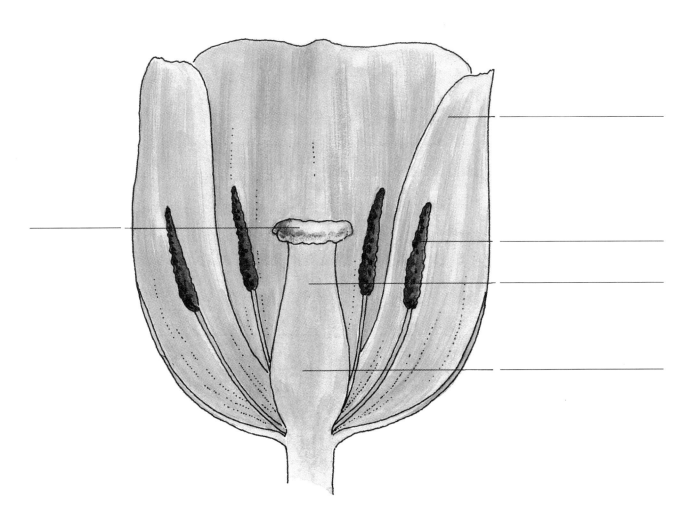

UNDERSTANDING SCIENCE BOOK 1 PAGE 101

Write a report of your experiment.

pull flower apart, tweezers, petal, sticky tape, stamen, stigma, ovary, style

Diagram

Method

_____
_____
_____
_____

Results

petal	stamen	stigma, style and ovary
	male part	female part

UNDERSTANDING SCIENCE BOOK 1 PAGE 140

Seed dispersal

Look at page 140.

Complete resource sheet 7.5.

Name the type of dispersal for each of the following:

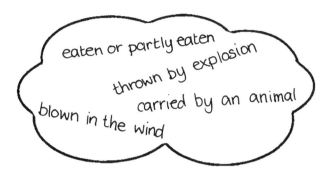
eaten or partly eaten
thrown by explosion
carried by an animal
blown in the wind

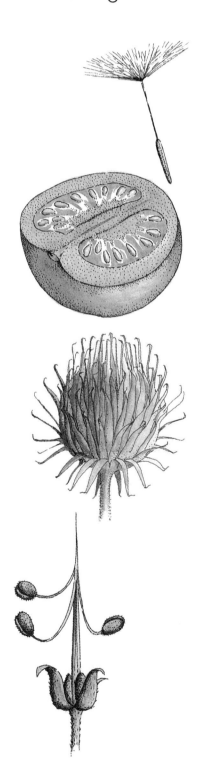

_____

_____

_____

_____

Readabout

UNDERSTANDING SCIENCE BOOK 1 PAGE 104

Konrad Lorenz

Read page 104.

Name: _____
Place of birth: _____
Year of birth: _____
Three interesting facts:
_____
_____
_____

Crossword

1 Time when an animal is able to reproduce.
2 Country where Lorenz was born.
3 Male sex cell in a flower.
4 Where female eggs in a flower are found.
5 When an egg and sperm meet.

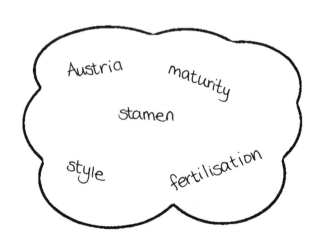

Austria   maturity   stamen   style   fertilisation

UNDERSTANDING SCIENCE BOOK 1 PAGES 92–104

Unit 7 test

Name _____ Form _____

1 Label the diagram.

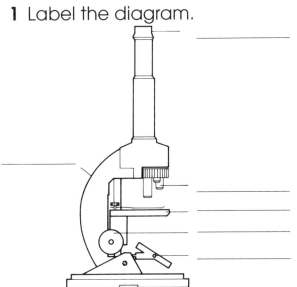
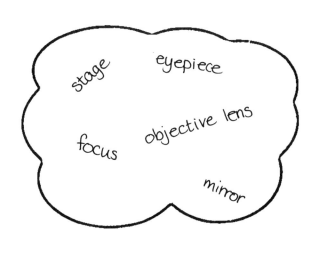

stage   eyepiece   focus   objective lens   mirror

2 If the slide under the microscope moves up, what do you see as you look down through the lens? Is it A, B, C or D?

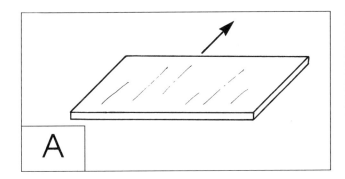
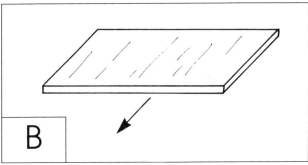
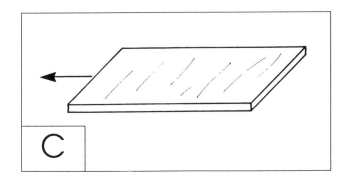
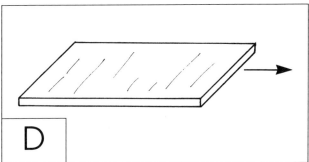

Answer _____

continued ➤

US 1 Support Material

UNDERSTANDING SCIENCE BOOK 1 PAGES 92–104

➤ continued

3 Name the following.

 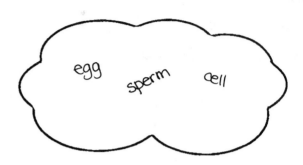

_____   _____

4 List the reproductive cycle in animals, starting with maturity.

1 Maturity

2 _____

3 _____

4 _____

5 _____

6 _____

5 Where are the male cells and female cells found in a flower? Is it A, B, C, D or E?

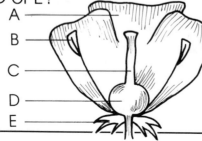

male cells (pollen) _____

female cells (egg cells) _____